Limerick County Library

30012 00614245 8

WITHDRAWN FROM STOCK

Seattle
day BY day™

1st Edition

by Beth Taylor

917·977

KU-190-197

WILEY
Wiley Publishing, Inc.

Limerick
County Library
0061424S

Contents

Published by:

Wiley Publishing, Inc.

111 River St.
Hoboken, NJ 07030-5774

Copyright © 2009 Wiley Publishing, Inc., Hoboken, New Jersey. All rights
reserved. No part of this publication may be reproduced, stored in a
retrieval system or transmitted in any form or by any means, electronic,
mechanical, photocopying, recording, scanning or otherwise, except as
permitted under Sections 107 or 108 of the 1976 United States Copyright
Act, without either the prior written permission of the Publisher, or
authorization through payment of the appropriate per-copy fee to the
Copyright Clearance Center, 222 Rosewood Drive, Danvers, MA 01923,
978/750-8400, fax 978/646-8600. Requests to the Publisher for permission should be addressed to the Legal Department, Wiley Publishing,
Inc., 10475 Crosspoint Blvd., Indianapolis, IN 46256, 317/572-3447, fax
317/572-4355, or online at http://www.wiley.com/go/permissions.

Wiley, the Wiley Publishing logo, and Day by Day are trademarks or registered trademarks of John Wiley & Sons, Inc. and/or its affiliates. Frommer's is a trademark or registered trademark of Arthur Frommer. Used
under license. All other trademarks are the property of their respective
owners. Wiley Publishing, Inc. is not associated with any product or ven-
dor mentioned in this book.

ISBN 978-0-470-28941-9

Editor: Linda Barth
Production Editor: Heather Wilcox
Photo Editor: Richard Fox
Cartographer: Elizabeth Puhl
Production by Wiley Indianapolis Composition Services

For information on our other products and services or to obtain technical
support, please contact our Customer Care Department within the U.S.
at 800/762-2974, outside the U.S. at 317/572-3993 or fax 317/572-4002.

Wiley also publishes its books in a variety of electronic formats. Some
content that appears in print may not be available in electronic formats.

Manufactured in China

5   4   3   2   1

A Note from the Publisher

Organizing your time. That's what this guide is all about.

Other guides give you long lists of things to see and do and then expect you to fit the pieces together. The Day by Day guides are different. These guides tell you the best of everything, and then they show you how to see it *in the smartest, most time-efficient way*. Our authors have designed detailed itineraries organized by time, neighborhood, or special interest. And each tour comes with a bulleted map that takes you from stop to stop.

Hoping to explore Seattle's iconic Pike Place Market or tour the city's eerie underground past? Want to try some of the country's finest coffee while strolling through Seattle's hip shopping districts? Whatever your interest or schedule, the Day by Days give you the smartest routes to follow. Not only do we take you to the top attractions, hotels, and restaurants, but we also help you access those special moments that locals get to experience—those "finds" that turn tourists into travelers.

The Day by Days are also your top choice if you're looking for one complete guide for all your travel needs. The best hotels and restaurants for every budget, the greatest shopping values, the wildest nightlife—it's all here.

Why should you trust our judgment? Because our authors personally visit each place they write about. They're an independent lot who say what they think and would never include places they wouldn't recommend to their best friends. They're also open to suggestions from readers. If you'd like to contact them, please send your comments my way at mspring@wiley.com, and I'll pass them on.

Enjoy your Day by Day guide—the most helpful travel companion you can buy. And have the trip of a lifetime.

Warm regards,

Michael Spring, Publisher
Frommer's Travel Guides

About the Author

Beth Taylor is an Air Force brat who roamed the world before finding her heart's home in Seattle. She's reported and edited at newspapers and magazines in Florida and the Pacific Northwest and written a variety of travel articles and guides. Degrees in journalism and political science have been helpful in understanding and describing the lands she's explored, but as any traveler knows, the tools that really count are curiosity and a sense of adventure.

Acknowledgments

Many thanks to Scott and Molly for joining in enthusiastically on many of my explorations and for their patience during the writing process. And much gratitude also goes to my editor, Linda Barth, whose unflappable, upbeat outlook kept the book on track and made the project a pleasure.

An Additional Note

Please be advised that travel information is subject to change at any time—and this is especially true of prices. We therefore suggest that you write or call ahead for confirmation when making your travel plans. The authors, editors, and publisher cannot be held responsible for the experiences of readers while traveling. Your safety is important to us, however, so we encourage you to stay alert and be aware of your surroundings.

Star Ratings, Icons & Abbreviations

Every hotel, restaurant, and attraction listing in this guide has been ranked for quality, value, service, amenities, and special features using a **star-rating system.** Hotels, restaurants, attractions, shopping, and nightlife are rated on a scale of zero stars (recommended) to three stars (exceptional). In addition to the star-rating system, we also use a **kids icon** to point out the best bets for families. Within each tour, we recommend cafes, bars, or restaurants where you can take a break. Each of these stops appears in a shaded box marked with a coffee-cup-shaped bullet ☕ .

The following **abbreviations** are used for credit cards:

AE	American Express	DISC	Discover	V	Visa
DC	Diners Club	MC	MasterCard		

Frommers.com

Now that you have this guidebook to help you plan a great trip, visit our web-site at **www.frommers.com** for additional travel information on more than 4,000 destinations. We update features regularly to give you instant access to the most current trip-planning information available. At Frommers.com, you'll find scoops on the best airfares, lodging rates, and car rental bargains. You can even book your travel online through our reliable travel booking partners. Other popular features include:

- Online updates of our most popular guidebooks
- Vacation sweepstakes and contest giveaways
- Newsletters highlighting the hottest travel trends
- Podcasts, interactive maps, and up-to-the-minute events listings
- Opinionated blog entries by Arthur Frommer himself
- Online travel message boards with featured travel discussions

A Note on Prices

In the "Take a Break" and "Best Bets" sections of this book, we have used a system of dollar signs to show a range of costs for 1 night in a hotel (the price of a double-occupancy room) or the cost of an entree at a restaurant. Use the following table to decipher the dollar signs:

Cost	Hotels	Restaurants
$	under $100	under $10
$$	$100–$200	$10–$20
$$$	$200–$300	$20–$30
$$$$	$300–$400	$30–$40
$$$$$	over $400	over $40

An Invitation to the Reader

In researching this book, we discovered many wonderful places—hotels, restaurants, shops, and more. We're sure you'll find others. Please tell us about them, so we can share the information with your fellow travelers in upcoming editions. If you were disappointed with a recommendation, we'd love to know that, too. Please write to:

Frommer's Seattle Day by Day 1st Edition
Wiley Publishing, Inc. • 111 River St. • Hoboken, NJ 07030-5774

16 Favorite
Moments

16 Favorite **Moments**

1. Flying fish at Pike Place Market
2. SkyCity restaurant
3. Fremont Troll
4. Underground Tour
5. Ferryboat
6. Climbing salmon
7. Bumbershoot
8. Tillicum Village
9. New Year's Eve at the Needle
10. Elliott Bay Book Company
11. Alki Beach
12. Lake Union kayak rental
13. Lake Union houseboats
14. Seafair at Alki Beach
15. Monorail
16. Original Starbucks

Caffeine-driven yet laid-back, practical yet dreamy, soggy yet obsessive about the great outdoors, Seattle is a land of extremes. Perched on the edge of the continent, this pioneer-spirited town has always reached toward the future. There's plenty of the old and the new here, from the former brothels of the Gold Rush era to the take-your-breath-away architecture of the Central Library. And where else will you find folks standing at a crosswalk in the pouring rain, nary a car in sight, clutching their lattes and waiting obediently for the crossing signal? Seattle is a quirky, endearing town, and here are a few of the best things about it.

1 **Dodging the flying fish.** Just behind Rachel, the giant piggybank that guards Seattle's beloved Pike Place Market, fishmongers noisily toss salmon across the counter and work the crowds that gather to watch them. Beware of the "snapping" monkfish—and the Pike Place Fish Market staffer hiding behind the counter, string in hand, waiting for the next unsuspecting tourist. *See p 54.*

2 **Spinning at the Space Needle.** On a clear day, head to the Space Needle's SkyCity revolving restaurant. You'll view the Emerald City from every angle as you rotate your way through lunch or dinner, and a

The Space Needle has become a Seattle icon.

trip to the observation deck is included in the price of your meal. Top it off with a fudgy Lunar Orbiter—complete with dry-ice Seattle "fog." *See p 123.*

3 **Climbing on the troll.** Hunkered under the Aurora Bridge in the funky Fremont neighborhood is a menacing, shaggy-haired troll, clutching an actual Volkswagen Beetle in his gnarled left hand. Ill-tempered he may be, but he's never harmed any of the tourists who scramble up for photo-ops. *See p 74.*

4 **Gawking at the view.** This is the drop-dead gorgeous view you've seen on all the postcards: the Seattle skyline, punctuated dramatically by the Space Needle, set against snow-frosted Mt. Rainier. Even if the mountain's not "out" (and it does often hide behind clouds), it's worth a visit to Kerry Park on Queen Anne Hill to see the rest. *See p 9.*

5 **Going down under.** Seattle wasn't always on the level—at least, not the one folks walk on today. Down below historic Pioneer Square, Underground Tour guides will lead you through subterranean passages that were once Seattle streets and relate spicy tales of the city's quirky and occasionally naughty early history. *See p 44.*

6 **Riding a ferryboat.** Gliding across the Puget Sound is one of the best ways to experience this city, which is all about water. The passengers tapping away on their laptops are local commuters, taking advantage of the free Wi-Fi. Grab a scone and a latte on board and enjoy. *See p 17*.

7 **Watching the fish climb.** At the Hiram M. Chittenden Locks, see the world's smartest salmon climb man-made ladders to get from the Puget Sound to the lakes and streams where the next generation will begin its own journey. While you're at it, stop and wave at the boats that are being raised up and down in the locks. It's a Seattle tradition. *See p 98*.

8 **Partying at Bumbershoot.** Seattle celebrates summer like nobody's business. The mother of all the non-stop festivals is Bumbershoot, held at the Seattle Center on Labor Day weekend to "welcome" back the rainy season. Expect most anything at eclectic Bumbershoot, from stilt-walkers to impromptu parades to sculptures made of "junk." *See p 96*.

9 **Savoring salmon at Tillicum Village.** The local Native Americans greeted Seattle's pioneer families warmly, and you can get a taste of

Consider scheduling your visit to coincide with Bumbershoot, Seattle's world-famous city-wide festival.

Ferryboats are a major part of life in Seattle, which has the most extensive ferry systems in the country.

that hospitality here. As your boat lands, you'll be handed a steaming bowl of clams, then set free to explore Blake Island while salmon roasts in the longhouse. During dinner, you're treated to a showcase of tribal dances and legends. The high-tech special effects are not exactly traditional, but they're pretty cool nonetheless. *See p 25*.

10 **Ringing in the New Year at the Needle.** You've never seen fireworks like these. Exuberant explosions of color "climb" their way up the Needle as festive music booms in the background. Get to Seattle Center around 10:30pm and stake out the highest spot you can find on the west side of the Center House, near the front. Then send someone inside to fetch hot cocoa and popcorn. *See p 9*.

11 **Curling up with a book at Elliott Bay Book Company.** Get lost in Seattle's favorite bookstore— easy to do in its labyrinth of floors and nooks. In the children's section, kids can climb into a castle to read. The downstairs cafe serves up lattes and tasty fare, and its walls are lined with books to be borrowed while you munch. *See p 84*.

12 **Soaking up the sun at Alki Beach.** The Denny Party knew a good thing when they saw it, which

No lawn-mowing is necessary at Seattle's famed houseboats.

is why they made Alki Beach the "Birthplace of Seattle" in 1851. Today, you can gaze across the Puget Sound at the Seattle skyline as you bike, skate, or walk along a 2-mile (3km) path skirting the sandy beach. Bikes, blades, and go-carts are available for rent. Word of warning: The water's chilly! *See p 17.*

⑬ Visiting the "neighbors." Rent a kayak and explore the charming floating "neighborhoods" on Lake Union. About 500 Seattleites live on the water, in boats of every size and shape—including the one featured in the movie *Sleepless in Seattle*. Just like any "city," there are some upscale areas and others populated by funky little vessels. *See p 17.*

⑭ Ogling the pirates. Seafair is a month of merriment and mischief, kicked off in early July by the Landing of the Pirates at Alki Beach. That's right, pirates. As in Vikings, whose blood coursed through the veins of Seattle's largely Scandinavian settlers. Nearly every neighborhood has its own Seafair festival. The zany Torchlight Parade in downtown Seattle is my personal favorite. *See p 96.*

⑮ Riding the monorail. Built for the 1962 World Fair, it's only a mile-long (1.5km) ride, but gliding above downtown is a true Seattle experience. The monorail starts at the Seattle Center and ends on the upper floor of the hip Westlake Mall. In between, you zoom through the middle of the bizarre but fascinating Experience Music Project, an innovative museum designed by Frank Gehry and inspired by Seattle native Jimi Hendrix. From the air, the EMP looks like a smashed guitar; from the ground, it's anyone's guess! *See p 9.*

⑯ Sipping lots of lattes. You can't get a better cuppa joe anywhere in the world than right here, where the nation's espresso craze began. Even if you don't know your double-tall-skinny-no-whip from your venti-soy-half-caff, it's fun to make a pilgrimage to the original Starbucks at Pike Place Market. It's standing-room-only, so carry your cup with you as you browse the market stalls. *See p 39.* ●

Glide through the super futuristic Experience Music Project on the monorail.

The Best in **One Day**

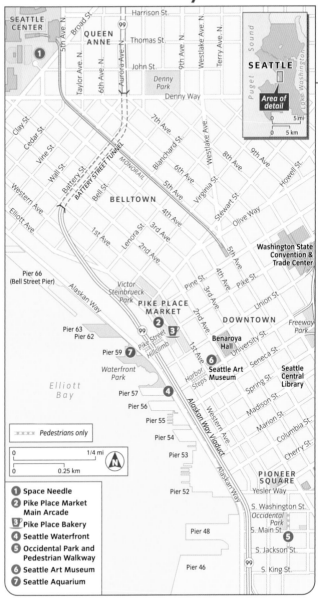

Area of detail

SEATTLE

Puget Sound

Lake Washington

0   5 mi
0   5 km

---- Pedestrians only

0   1/4 mi
0   0.25 km

1 Space Needle
2 Pike Place Market Main Arcade
3 Pike Place Bakery
4 Seattle Waterfront
5 Occidental Park and Pedestrian Walkway
6 Seattle Art Museum
7 Seattle Aquarium

O **ne of the safest and most compact big cities in the country,** Seattle is easy—and just plain fun—to navigate on foot. This sampler-platter tour roams from one end of town to the other. But don't worry too much about tiring yourself out. There are plenty of places to rest your weary feet while enjoying the eclectic street scene. START: **Monorail or bus 1, 2, 3, 4, 13, 15, 16, or 18 to Seattle Center.**

1 ★★★ kids **Space Needle.** Part retro, part futuristic, and more than a touch eccentric, the Needle is the perfect symbol for Seattle. It was built for the World's Fair in 1962 after an artist sketched out a space-age focal point for the event on a placemat at—where else?—a local coffee shop. Lines for the glass elevator ride up to the observation deck can be long in summertime, but it's worth the wait—just try not to get shoved to the back, or you'll miss the view on the way up. If you go in the winter and it happens to be snowing (a rare event), you'll be moving faster than the flakes, which will seem to be falling upward. If, more likely, it's raining, don't let that stop you. The typical Seattle mist only makes the view from the top that much dreamier. You can also have lunch or dinner at the revolving SkyCity restaurant (reservations highly recommended) and rotate around the town while you dine. Best of all, your elevator ride to the top is free if you're dining at

SkyCity. 🕐 *1 hr. Summer weekends are busiest. 400 Broad St.* 📞 *206/ 905-2180. www.spaceneedle.com. Observation deck tickets $16 adults, $14 seniors, $8 ages 4–13. Sun–Thurs 9am–11pm; Fri–Sat 9am–noon.*

2 ★★★ kids **Pike Place Market Main Arcade.** Here it is: home of those famous flying fish, which you can't help but see (better duck!) right behind Rachel, the beloved porcine statue. With 1 day in town, you won't have time to go Down Under (p. 58), but there's plenty to overwhelm the senses on the Market's top floor. Street

Even if you're not normally a fan of seafood, the fresh fish at Pike Place Market are hard to resist.

musicians turn junk into instruments, farmers hawk a spectacular assortment of locally grown produce—much of which you'll enjoy at Seattle's finest restaurants—and local artists

Travel Tip

Despite Seattle's walkability, there are times when your feet just need a break. To get downtown from Seattle Center—home of the Space Needle (see **1** above)—hop on the monorail ($4 round-trip for adults, $1.50 ages 5–12, $2 for seniors) for the short ride to Westlake Center. From there, take a free metro bus anywhere in the downtown, Pioneer Square, Pike Place Market, and waterfront neighborhoods. The historic waterfront trolley has been temporarily halted for maintenance upgrades, but Waterfront Streetcar Line buses (painted to look like trolleys) do the job for now. Better yet, they're free.

Pike Place Market is far more than a farmer's market and is well worth exploring.

display their eclectic talents. The Market is a great place to pick up high-quality souvenirs to suit any budget. But my weakness is the enormous bouquets of flowers, fresh from the fields in nearby lush valleys, and costing half what you'd pay at a grocery store for a punier spray. ⏱ *1 hr. Pike Place & Pike St.* ☎ *206/682-7453. www.pikeplacemarket.org. Mon–Sat 10am–6pm; Sun 11am–5pm.*

3 **Pike Place Bakery.** It's almost impossible to walk through the Market without sampling some of the wares. Go ahead, give in to the urge! Bite into a creamy blueberry Danish or a spicy cinnamon crispy at this popular bakery. Be sure to check for the daily special. *1501 Pike Place.* ☎ *206/682-2829. www.pikeplacebakery.com. $.*

4 ★★ kids **Seattle Waterfront.** Head to Seattle's sparkling Elliott Bay, where you can walk from pier to pier and watch the cruise ships come and go. The waterfront is always lively, and the smell is a pleasant mix of salt water and fresh fish and chips, available at stands along the way. If you have little ones, a stop at Pier 57's Bay Pavilion is a must. Pirates Plunder gift shop has every kind of sea-scalawag item imaginable; at the

back of the pavilion, an antique carousel and game room offer a fun break. But the Harbor is not all about play; it's a real working waterfront, one of the busiest in the nation. The best way to see it in action is to get out on the water. **Argosy Cruises** (Pier 55, Seattle Waterfront; ☎ 206/623-1445; www.argosycruises.com) offers hour-long harbor tours—along with a variety of other dinner and pleasure cruises—on boats leaving from Pier 55. The harbor tour leaves at 1:30pm every day, and varying additional times depending on the day and season. $15 Jan–Mar and Oct–Dec; $19 April–Sept for adults; $6.45 Jan–Mar and Oct–Dec and $7.80 April–Sept for ages 5–12. If you don't have time for a tour, stop by **Waterfront Park,** which stretches between Piers 57 and 61, and peer out at the bay through free telescopes. ⏱ *1 hr.*

5 **Occidental Park and Pedestrian Walkway.** From the waterfront, walk or take the free Route 99 bus (it's the one that's painted to look like a trolley) to Jackson St. and Occidental Ave. The bricked walkway occupies 1 block; the park claims the block to the north. In this area you'll find a sampling of Seattle's avant-garde art galleries; Victorian-Romanesque buildings constructed hurriedly during the Gold Rush; and Glasshouse Studio (311 Occidental Ave. S.; ☎ 206/682-9939; www.glasshouse-studio.com), where you can watch skilled glassblowers at their craft. Several totem poles tower over visitors, and the Fallen Firefighter's Memorial pays tribute to those who have lost their lives battling fires throughout Seattle's history. ⏱ *1 hr. Occidental Ave. & Jackson St.*

The Seattle Aquarium offers a view into life in Puget Sound.

6 ★★★ Seattle Art Museum. SAM's eclectic global collections include Northwest Native American, Pan-Asian, African, European, and American modern art. The special exhibits are always worth perusing, and there are lots of activities for kids in conjunction with the displays. Despite its world-class reputation, this museum has a friendly feel, and a staff that is passionate about art and treats visitors as honored guests. The gift shop is one of the best you'll find. SAM's permanent collections are on display free the first Thursday of every month; and they are free for teens the second Friday of each month. ⏱ *2 hr. 1300 1st Ave. ☎ 206/654-3100. www.seattleartmuseum.org. Admission $13 adults, $10 seniors over 62, $7 students & kids 13–17, free for kids 12 & under. Tues–Sun 10am–5pm; Thurs–Fri 10am–9pm.*

7 ★★ kids Seattle Aquarium. Recently expanded to the tune of $41 million, this is a sealife-lover's dream come true. The aquarium's pride and joy, a 40×20-foot (12×6m) viewing window, gives visitors a glimpse of the creatures that swim in the Puget Sound. Divers interact with fish in the tank several times a day, while volunteers explain what's going on. The aquarium, by the way, is perched on a pier overhanging the Sound, so many of these animals are also swimming under your feet. Don't miss the giant Pacific octopus—the largest in the world—as well as the entertaining sea otters and the Underwater Dome, which gives you a 360-degree view of an enormous tank filled with sharks and other interesting creatures. ⏱ *2 hr. 1483 Alaskan Way on Pier 59. ☎ 206/386-4300. www.seattle aquarium.org. Admission is $15 adults, $10 ages 4–12. Daily 9:30am–5pm.*

Good Deal

A CityPass (☎ 888/330-5008; www.citypass.com) is one of the best deals is town. You can visit five popular Seattle destinations for half the regular price (that's assuming, of course, that you take them all in within 9 days). Better yet, you won't have to wait in line; just breeze on in with your ticket in hand. The passes will get you into the Seattle Aquarium, Pacific Science Center, Museum of Flight, and Woodland Park Zoo—and onto an Argosy Cruises boat for an entertaining tour of Elliott Bay. A CityPass costs $44 for adults and $29 for kids ages 3–12. You can buy them at any of the included attractions, or order them ahead from the website.

The Best in **Two Days**

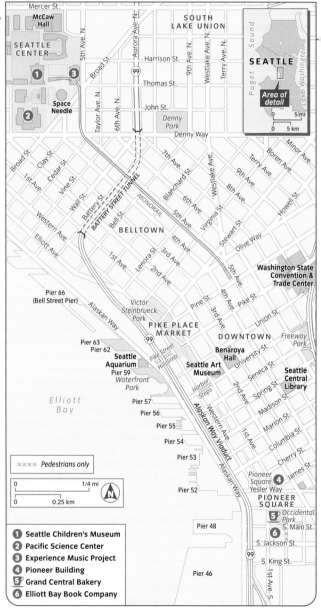

1 Seattle Children's Museum
2 Pacific Science Center
3 Experience Music Project
4 Pioneer Building
5 Grand Central Bakery
6 Elliott Bay Book Company

Pedestrians only

The first day was the smorgasbord tour of Seattle highlights; now it's time to go back and spend some quality time in two of the city's most interesting areas: Seattle Center and Pioneer Square.
START: **Monorail or bus 1, 2, 3, 4, 13, 15, 16, or 18 to Seattle Center.**

① ★ kids Seattle Children's Museum. Inside the Center House, near the Space Needle at Seattle Center, you'll see the children's museum below, visible through a railed opening in the floor. The bright colors and enchanted forest are irresistible to kids, so hop on the glass elevator (near the back of the Center House) and ride downstairs to the museum. The emphasis is on nature and multicultural learning, with crafts, exhibits, and activities that turn education into play for kids from birth to age 10. ⏱ *90 min. 305 Harrison St.* ☎ *206/441-1768.*

The dinosaurs that prowl the Pacific Science Center are fun for kids and adults alike.

www.thechildrensmuseum.org. Admission is $7.50 for adults & children, free for kids under age 1. Mon–Fri 10am–5pm; Sat–Sun 10am–6pm.

② ★★ kids Pacific Science Center. Do touch! is the rule at this museum at Seattle Center. Though interesting for all ages, this is really a youth-focused museum. A great deal of effort has gone into making nearly every exhibit a hands-on experience. Kids love the anima-tronic dinosaurs, the butterfly garden, and the Body Works area, where they can test their own physical abilities. There are animals to touch, a playground for tiny tots, and usually a special exhibit of bubbles, snakes, or something else sure to engage. You can gaze at the stars in the planetarium, and the laser shows on Thursday, Friday, and Saturday nights are set to music by bands like the Beatles and Led Zeppelin. The center's IMAX theaters show movies for varying ages. ⏱ *2 hr. 200 2nd Ave. N.* ☎ *206/443-2844. www.pacsci.org. Mon–Fri 10am–5pm; Sat–Sun 10am–6pm. Admission $11 adults, $9.50 seniors, $8 ages 6–12, $6 ages 3–5. IMAX $8–$11 adults, $7.50–$9.50 seniors, $7–$8.50 ages 6–12, $6 ages 3–5, discounts available for combination passes.*

③ ★ Experience Music Project/Science Fiction Museum & Hall of Fame. Microsoft billionaire Paul Allen's monument to Seattle's own rock legend, Jimi Hendrix, this museum is fascinating for music-lovers of all

Be sure to explore the remains of old Seattle, which lie a full story beneath the modern city, on the Underground Tour.

beneath the sidewalks to view the remnants of the original pioneer town, a full story lower than the rebuilt city. (It seems there was a little problem with sewage coming back in with the tides.) You'll get a 90-minute lowdown (literally) on the era's get-rich-quick schemers, gold-crazy prospectors, and colorful women who listed their occupation as "seamstress," though they seldom produced a stitch. Some of the content is mature, but it should go right over the heads of the little ones. In any case, they are more fascinated by the stories of the rats which once roamed the streets. The guides are very funny, and they know their stuff. ⏲ *90 min. 1st Ave. & Yesler Way. Underground Tour, 610 1st Ave. #200.* ☎ *206/682-4646. www.undergroundtour.com. $14 adults, $7 children 7–12. Tours offered daily, throughout the day.*

ages. There are tons of interactive exhibits on popular music—from soul to rock to hip-hop—including the chance to record your own CD in the Jam Studio, using guitars, drums, keyboard, and voice. Technology makes it possible even if you've never played an instrument. And the Science Fiction Museum is worth a look, too, if you're interested in the genre. Both are housed in a stunning Frank Gehry–designed building meant to look from above like one of Jimi's guitars. From the street, it looks more like an undulating blob of metal. Either way, it's worth a peek even if you're not a music fan. ⏲ *90 min. 325 5th Ave. N. (at Seattle Center).* ☎ *206/770-2700. www.empsfm. org. Admission to both $15 adults, $12 seniors/ages 5–17, free for kids under 5. Daily 10am–5pm.*

④ ★★ **Pioneer Building.** This historic grand dame now houses Doc Maynard's Pub and the popular Underground Tour, which takes you

Music-lovers and fans of modern architecture will both find something to love at the Experience Music Project.

5 ★ Grand Central Bakery.

Some of the best bread in this dough-loving town comes from this gem of a bakery, which you can enter from Occidental Park or the Grand Central Arcade on 1st Ave. My advice? Gobble down a sweet potato galette (topped with sugared pecans) while you're there, and take home an epi baguette, slightly sweet and shaped in a distinctive zigzag pattern. *214 1st Ave. S.* ☎ *206/622-3644. $.*

Rest your weary feet while snacking on some of Seattle's best baked goods at Grand Central Bakery.

Get in from the rain at the Elliott Bay Book Company, housed in a Gold Rush–era building.

6 ★★★ Elliott Bay Book Company.

Walking the creaky wooden floors of this historic building feels like paying a visit to Seattle's living room. And no wonder: Seattleites love to while away the hours here. During the Gold Rush this building housed the Globe Hotel. Now it houses more than 150,000 books. Your challenge: not to bring home more than you can fit in your carry-on! ⏱ *30 min. 101 S. Main St.* ☎ *206/624-6600. www.elliottbay book.com. Mon–Sat 9:30am–10pm, Sun 11am–7pm.*

Seattle Makes Music

The Kingsmen, Jimi Hendrix, Heart, Queensrÿche, Pearl Jam, Nirvana, Alice in Chains, Death Cab for Cutie, Modest Mouse—Seattle just seems to spawn great music. Since the 1950s, the Emerald City has been famous for its garage bands that end up going big-time. The "Louie Louie" phenomenon began when the Wailers from Tacoma (just south of Seattle) recorded the song in 1960 and it became a radio hit. (A couple of years later, two Northwest bands from a bit farther south—Portland, Oregon—recorded the same song: the Kingsmen and Paul Revere and the Raiders.) In the early 1990s, Seattle's Kurt Cobain and his band Nirvana kicked off the grunge era that made Seattle arguably the hippest place on the planet. Today's Seattle rockers, like Modest Mouse, may be a bit less well known, but they're no less exciting.

The Best in **Three Days**

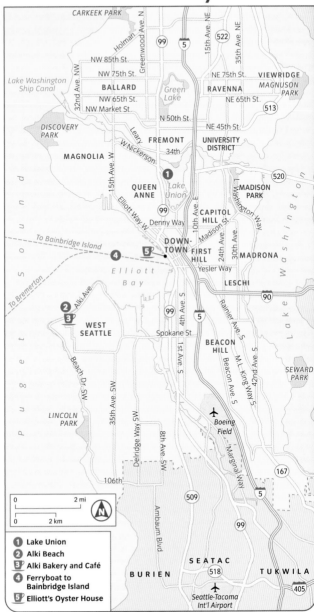

1 Lake Union
2 Alki Beach
3 Alki Bakery and Café
4 Ferryboat to Bainbridge Island
5 Elliott's Oyster House

You can't fully appreciate Seattle without getting out on the water. After all, nearly half the Emerald City is immersed in the stuff! Today, start out by giving your feet a break and letting your arms do all the work. Then relax with some more restful water activities. START: **Bus 16, 26, or 28 to Lake Union.**

1 ★★ Boating Lake Union. There's nothing quite like paddling a boat right in the heart of a city. Seaplanes gracefully take off and land as you explore the houseboat "neighborhoods" and soak in the dramatic view of the Space Needle and Seattle's distinctive skyline. If you want to pay for the extra rental time, you can paddle right up to the dock at several restaurants and stop for lunch. ⏱ *90 min. Boats may be rented at several locations, including the Center for Wooden Boats (1010 Valley St.; ☎ 206/382-2628; rowboats & sailboats from $15 per hour), which also has a fascinating collection of historic boats & offers a free sailboat ride at 2pm Sun. To rent a kayak try the Northwest Outdoor Center (2100 Westlake Ave. N, Ste. 1; ☎ 206/281-9694; kayak rentals $12 per hour single or $17 per hour double). Lessons are available.*

2 ★★★ Alki Beach. This is the best beach in Seattle—though technically, it's in West Seattle. The mood is always festive, the view of Elliott Bay and the Seattle skyline is breathtaking, and the water is always—even in the summertime— very chilly. From the spring through the fall, you can zip across Elliott Bay from the Seattle Waterfront on the water taxi. In the wintertime, you'll need to drive over the West Seattle Bridge and take the Harbor Ave/Avalon Way exit, then turn right onto Harbor Avenue and bear left at Alki Ave. This wide, sandy beach has a promenade for walkers, joggers, and roller-bladers, and you can rent bikes or go-carts at shops across from the beach. Shops and cafes line the street across from the water, so you need never go hungry. ⏱ *2 hr.*

3 Alki Bakery and Cafe. If all the salty air makes you long for something sweet, take a beach break for pastries and coffee. You can also get more substantial fare here: sandwiches, pasta, or seafood. Enjoy your snack outside, with the panoramic ocean and mountain views thrown in for free! *2738 Alki Ave. SW. ☎ 206/935-1352. $.*

4 ★★ Ferryboat to Bainbridge Island. Washington State runs the largest ferry system in the

Don't miss getting an up-close view of the charming houseboats.

country, and this line is very popular with commuters. You could plug in your laptop and check e-mail for free, but don't do it. Instead, grab a cup of coffee and a raspberry scone at the onboard cafe, then head out on deck and enjoy the 35-minute ride. If you walk onto the ferry, arrive 15 minutes before departure time; if you drive your car on (not recommended), come at least 20–30 minutes ahead. Drive-on wait times can be much longer during rush hours. ⏱ *1 hr. round-trip. Catch the ferryboat at the Seattle Ferry Terminal at Pier 52.* 📞 *206/464-6400 (from Seattle);* 📞 *206/464-6400 (from out-of-state). www.wsdot.wa.gov/ferries. Fares $6.70 for adults, $3.35 for seniors, $5.40 for children, $12 for car & driver. Check schedules for departure times.*

⑤ ★★ **Walk Through Winslow.** Once you've arrived on Bainbridge Island, follow the crowds walking into the charming town of Winslow, where you can roam the art galleries, taste some wine, and do some shopping on **Winslow Way.** A great place to see the work of hundreds of area artists—both new and seasoned—is the non-profit gallery **Bainbridge Arts and Crafts** (151 Winslow Way E.; 📞 206/842-3132; Mon–Sat 10am–6pm, Sun 11am–5pm). For a great cup of java, turn left (toward the water) at Madison Avenue South, then right onto Parfitt Way Southeast, and stroll over to **Pegasus Coffee House and Gallery,** a picturesque, ivy-covered brick shop on the waterfront that roasts its own tasty beans. ⏱ *2 hr.*

⑥ ★★ **Elliott's Oyster House.** Once you're back in Seattle, this is a great place to stop for fresh local seafood. Or head for the raw bar if you just need an oyster fix. It's the perfect place to wrap up a day on the water. *1201 Alaskan Way, Pier 56.* 📞 *206/623-4340. www.elliotts oysterhouse.com. $$. See p 117.* ●

Riding the ferry is half the fun of a trip to Bainbridge Island.

Seattle **Heritage**

1 Museum of Flight
2 Klondike Gold Rush International Historical Park
3 Wing Luke Asian Museum
4 Museum of History & Industry
5 Burke Museum of History and Culture
6 Nordic Heritage Museum
7 Café Besalu
8 Tillicum Village

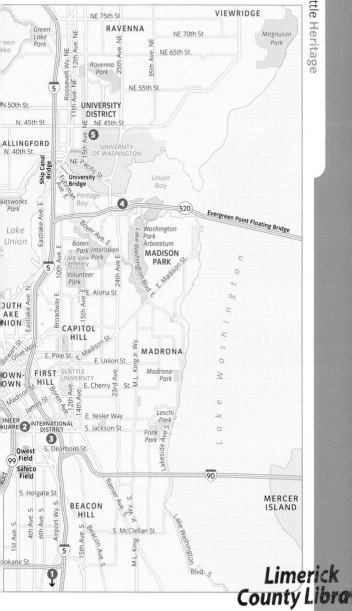

When it comes to historic roots, Seattle can't compare to a place like Boston, but the Emerald City has such a colorful, spirited past that it's hard not to get caught up in the fun. This tour will take you on a journey from the days before the arrival of Europeans to the birth of the aerospace industry that helped modern Seattle take flight. START: **Bus 174 to the Museum of Flight.**

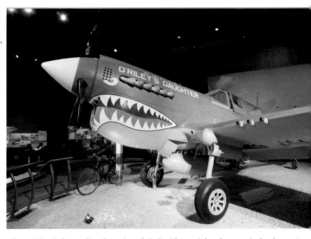

The aviation industry played a major role in Seattle's social and economic development.

1 ★★★ kids **Museum of Flight.** The focus here is the contemporary era—relatively speaking, since the history of aviation goes back pretty far in Seattle. This top-flight museum will amaze anyone remotely intrigued by the human species' determination to escape the bonds of earth. In the historic Red Barn (Boeing's first manufacturing building), you'll find exhibits on early American aviation, including the mail bag carried by William E. Boeing and Eddie Hubbard on the first international U.S. Air Mail flight, which went from Vancouver, B.C., to Seattle in 1919. The exhibit ends with the Boeing 707, which ushered in the jet age. The cavernous Great Gallery features dozens of historic aircraft, many of them hanging from the ceiling as though in flight. Visitors can climb into the cockpit of a real Blackbird, the fastest jet ever made. The Personal Courage Wing tells the stories of fighter aviators in World Wars I and II. And at the Airpark, you can view legendary aircraft including the Concorde and the country's first jet Air Force One. I especially love the simulator exhibit, which allows users to try (virtually) flying a plane and hang gliding. You can even try linking up with the Hubble Telescope. ⏱ *90 min.* ☎ *206/764-5720. www.museumofflight.org. 9404 E. Marginal Way S. $14 adults, $13 seniors, $7.50 ages 5–17, free 4 & under. Free 1st Thurs of every month from 5–9pm. Daily 10am–5pm.*

2 ★ kids **Klondike Gold Rush International Historical Park.** You're bound to catch Gold Fever as you listen to the tales of the Yukon-bound prospectors and their families

Seattle Takes Shape

In 1852, a windy, rain-drenched winter prompted Seattle's founders to move from Alki Point (now in West Seattle), where they had landed the previous year, to the better sheltered eastern shore of Elliott Bay. The reason for the zany layout of the town they created—now the Pioneer Square neighborhood—was the lack of agreement among the city fathers (and possibly the chronic drunkenness of at least one) as to which direction the roads should go. Perhaps not surprisingly, squabbling over roads has since become a Seattle tradition. Thirty-five years later, Seattle struck it rich when gold was discovered in the Yukon. Would-be prospectors stocked up on supplies before they headed out to the gold fields; on the way back, those who had struck it rich dropped a large percentage of their profits here. After a fire destroyed much of the downtown in 1889, Seattle's businessmen, frantic at missing out on profits, scrambled to rebuild their city. They built fast, but they built to last.

who passed through Seattle, and view personal items they left along the way. This is not only a museum but a national park (which also has a Canadian branch). Kids can earn honest-to-gosh Junior Ranger badges by filling in an activity book based on information gleaned from the two floors of exhibits. This keeps them conveniently busy while the grown-ups enjoy the displays. Films on the Gold Rush and Seattle's role in the mania are shown frequently. In the summer months, you can watch gold-panning demonstrations twice a day or take an afternoon walking tour of Pioneer Square, led by a park ranger. 🕐 *1 hr. 319 2nd Ave. S.* ☎ *206/220-4240. www.nps.gov/klse. Free admission. Daily 9am–5pm.*

At the interactive Klondike Gold Rush International Historical Park you'll learn everything you ever wanted to know about the Gold Rush.

Explore the influence of Asian immigrants to Seattle at the Wing Luke Asian Museum.

3 ★★ Wing Luke Asian Museum. Celebrating the diverse Asian cultures that have emigrated to the Pacific Northwest, the main exhibit here is "One Song Many Voices," which tells the 200-year-old story of Asians and Pacific Islanders settling in Washington state. Perhaps the most moving exhibit is "Camp Harmony D-4-44," a re-creation of a livestock stall converted into a family holding cell, barbed wire and all, from the Puyallup Fairgrounds just south of Seattle. The fairgrounds were used as an assembly area for Japanese Americans on their way to internment camps in 1942. The museum moved into new, much expanded quarters in the historic East Kong Yick Building, former home of the Freeman Hotel, in early 2008. ⏱ 1 hr. New location: 719 S. King St. (S. King St. & 8th Ave. S.). ☎ 206/623-5124. www.wingluke. org. $4 adults, $3 seniors & students, $2 ages 5–12. Tues–Fri 11am–4:30pm; Sat–Sun noon–4pm.

4 ★★ Museum of History & Industry (MOHAI). It may not have the most exciting name, but there is nothing dull about this museum. It's a great way to learn about Northwest history through riveting, often hands-on exhibits and historic photos. You can amble along the "sidewalks" of pre-fire Seattle, soon to be reduced to ashes by the Great Fire of 1889. And don't miss the exhibit on the blaze, which includes the very glue pot believed to have started the fire. ⏱ 1 hr. 2700 24th Ave E. ☎ 206/324-1126. www.seattlehistory.org. $7 adults, $5 ages 5–17 & seniors, free 4 & under. Also, free 1st Thurs of the month. Daily 10am–5pm; 1st Thurs of the month 10am–8pm.

5 ★★ Burke Museum of Natural History and Culture. I love this museum because it's small, doable in a couple of hours, and it has everything Washington: from 40-million-year-old fossils to an extensive Native American arts collection. Located on the tree-lined campus of the University of Washington, the Burke appeals to kids and adults alike. Dino Times, with its dinosaur skeletons and walk-through volcano, is enormously fun, and even the cultural showcases are both engaging and entertaining. ⏱ 1 hr. 17th Ave. NE & NE 45th St. ☎ 206/543-5590. www.washington. edu/burkemuseum. $8 adults, $6.50 seniors, $5 students & youth, free under 5. Daily 10am–5pm. Free 1st Thurs of the month.

6 ★ Nordic Heritage Museum. Unassuming but worthwhile, this two-story museum is the only one in the country that celebrates the history of the five Nordic countries, many of whose descendants call the Pacific Northwest home. My favorite exhibit brings to life the arrival of early Scandinavian immigrants, via Ellis Island, in the land of their dreams. You can feel the excitement, then the chaos and confusion of their new adventure. Each country—Denmark, Finland, Iceland, Norway, and Sweden—has a room at the museum to tell its story and show off its art and culture. Lots of kids' programs are offered, as well as classes in Nordic folk arts. ⏲ 1 hr. 3014 NW 67th St. ☎ 206/789-5707. www.nordicmuseum.org. $6 adults, $5 seniors & students, $5 children over 5. Tues–Sat 10am–4pm; Sun noon–4pm.

Learn about Seattle's past, including the Great Fire that destroyed much of the city, at the Museum of History & Industry.

7 ★ Café Besalu. The pain au chocolat here is melt-in-your-mouth delicious, as are the flaky croissants. For a more substantial snack, the quiches are yummy. Try to avoid the morning breakfast rush; the lines can be long at this popular neighborhood bakery. 5909 24th Ave. NW (at Market). ☎ 206/789-1463. $.

8 ★★★ kids Tillicum Village. Rewind to pre-European times in the Northwest at this Native American village. The local Indian tribes may have lived to regret their initial hospitality to the white settlers who landed at Alki Point and who, many years later, drove the Native Americans onto second-rate reservation land. But at Tillicum Village, the hospitality is in full force as a number of local tribes cooperatively present a salmon bake in the Longhouse, then a variety of traditional dances illustrating creation stories. Afterward, watch skilled tribal artists carving masks and other items, many of which can be purchased. The setting is lovely, forested Blake Island, believed to be an ancient campground of the Duwamish and Suquamish tribes, and the likely birthplace of Chief Seattle. There is a playground for children on Blake Island, and keep your camera handy, as more than likely you'll spot a few deer. Now a state park, it can be reached only by boat. ⏲ 4 hr. ☎ 206/933-8600. www.tillicum village.com. Argosy Cruises offers rides to & from Tillicum Village, leaving from Pier 55 on the Seattle waterfront. Price with cruise $80 adults, $73 seniors, $30 ages 5–12, free age 4 & under; dates & times vary by month.

Seattle for Art Lovers

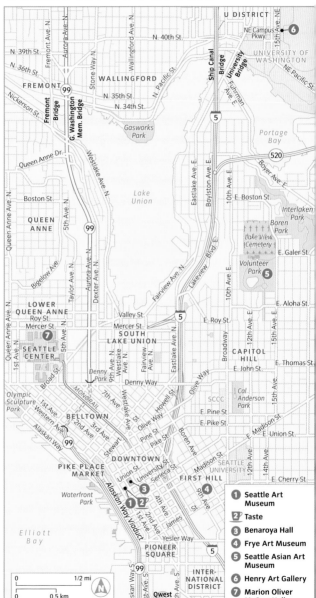

1 Seattle Art Museum
2 Taste
3 Benaroya Hall
4 Frye Art Museum
5 Seattle Asian Art Museum
6 Henry Art Gallery
7 Marion Oliver McCaw Hall

The Emerald City has always supported the arts with its extra cash, whether earned from gold, aerospace, or dot.com mania. Over the past decade or so, many new facilities have sprung up around town and older ones have solved their growing pains with grandiose expansions. This tour will give you a good look at just how diverse the Seattle art scene really is. START: **Bus 1, 2, 3, 4, 13, 15, 16, 18, 21, 22, 26, 28, or 358 to Union St.**

The Hammering Man looms over the Seattle Art Museum.

1 ★★★ Seattle Art Museum. You'll know you're there when you see the hardworking Hammering Man, a 48-foot (15m) tribute to the working classes who shaped Seattle's character. Appropriately, the arm of the animated outdoor sculpture, designed by Jonathan Borofsky, gets a rest every year on Labor Day. Inside, the recently expanded museum has two beautiful floors of free public space, including the Brotman Forum, which features changing exhibits and Cai Guo-Qiang's fanciful sculpture of nine cars falling across the space. ⏱ *2 hr. 1300 1st Ave.* ☎ *206/654-3100. www.seattleartmuseum.org. Admission $13 adults, $10 seniors over 62,*

$7 students & kids 13–17, free for kids 12 & under. Tues–Sun 10am–5pm; Thurs–Fri 10am–9pm. See p 65.

2 ★ Taste. The new cafe at the Seattle Art Museum serves fresh, creative dishes. You can grab a cup of espresso, indulge in a homemade s'more, or sit down to a duck confit. And those outrageously delicious veggies on your plate? They're all locally grown. Prices are reasonable and the menu includes kids' meals. *1300 1st Ave.* ☎ *206/903-5291. Tues–Sun 11am–10pm. $$.*

3 ★★ Benaroya Hall. Home to the Seattle Symphony, the Benaroya is aesthetically and acoustically state of the art. Check the website for concert and speaking dates. If you have children, check out the Tiny Tots and Discover Music! Performances. Even

World-famous glass artist Dale Chihuly designed the dramatic chandeliers at Benroya Hall.

Olympic Sculpture Park

You won't have to be cooped up indoors to enjoy the latest addition to Seattle's art scene, which opened to great acclaim in 2007. Run by the Seattle Art Museum, the **Olympic Sculpture Park** (2901 Western Ave.; ☎ 206/654-3100) is a unique outdoor sculpture park that features 9 acres (3.5 hectares) of very large permanent and traveling exhibits. Added bonus: It's all right on the waterfront. From *Father and Son*, a double fountain by Louise Bourgeois that captures a sometimes problematic relationship; to *Typewriter Eraser* by Claes Oldenburg and Coosje van Bruggen, a giant version of an old-fashioned everyday object (on loan through 2009), the creations are both fanciful and thought-provoking. Admission is free, and the park is open daily from 30 minutes before sunrise to 30 minutes after sunset.

if you can't attend a concert, the hall is worth a stop to ogle its dazzling, spiraling glass chandeliers, which were designed by world-famous Seattle glass artist Dale Chihuly. ⏱ *30 min. 200 University St.* ☎ *206/ 215-4800. www.seattlesymphony.org. Ticket prices vary; free admission to see the chandeliers.*

④ ★ **Frye Art Museum.** Charles and Emma Frye, German immigrants who made their fortune in gold-mad 19th-century Seattle, left their

Kids are welcome to climb on the stone camels outside the Seattle Asian Art Museum.

immense collection of then-contemporary art to the city to be displayed in one location. Thus was born the Frye. Its collected representational works—portraits, still lifes, landscapes—are by 19th- and 20th-century French, German, and American painters. But in recent years, the museum has re-invented itself, adding modern and abstract art to the collection. These new works are often intriguingly juxtaposed with paintings that once hung in the Frye's living room or meathouse. Recent exhibits include a show of drawings by underground cartoonist R. Crumb. ⏱ *1 hr. 704 Terry Ave.* ☎ *206/622-9250. www.fryeart.org. As mandated by Charles Frye, admission is free. Tues–Sat 10–5pm; Sun noon–5pm; Thurs open until 8pm.*

⑤ ★ **Seattle Asian Art Museum.** Set in the middle of lovely Volunteer Park (p 67) and operated by the Seattle Art Museum, SAAM features a stunning collection of historic and contemporary art from a variety of Asian cultures. If you love Eastern art—or want to learn more about it—this is the perfect venue. Most of the exhibits won't appeal greatly to younger kids, but they love playing in the child-size Japanese house. Shoes off first, of course! Don't miss (it would be hard to) Isamu Noguchi's captivating Black Sun sculpture outside the museum. A photo of the Space Needle taken through the statue's open center makes a great souvenir. 🕐 1 hr. 1400 E. Prospect St. ☎ 206/654-3100. www.seattleartmuseum.org. $5 adults; $3 seniors, students, & ages 13–17; free for kids 12 & under. Tues–Sun 10am–5pm; Thurs 10am–9pm; free 1st Thurs & 1st Sat of every month.

⑥ ★★ **Henry Art Gallery.** Old world meets new at the Henry, where you can find works by masters such as Rembrandt, but also avant-garde photography and sculpture. The Henry's solid reputation has soared since its mega-expansion a few years ago. One of its most popular permanent exhibits is James Turrell's riveting Skyspace, which turns light—both natural and artificial—into ever-changing art. 🕐 1 hr. University of Washington campus, 15th Ave. NE & NE 41st St. ☎ 206/221-4980. www.henryart.org. Admission $10 adults, $6 seniors, free for students & ages 13 & under. Tues–Sun 11am–5pm; Thurs until 8pm.

⑦ ★ **Marion Oliver McCaw Hall.** Seattle has seen a burgeoning of art houses and expansions since the '90s, and this was one of the

Statues of dancers adorn the lobby of Marion Oliver McCaw Hall.

most notable. Home to the Seattle Opera and the Pacific Northwest Ballet, the hall—resplendent with color and drama—opened in 2003 to rave reviews for its architectural beauty, acoustic excellence, and stunning art exhibits. Outside, a contemporary fountain blends in seamlessly with the walkway; at night, colored lights create swirls of color. If you're in town over the holidays, the PNB's Nutcracker—complete with Where the Wild Things Are author Maurice Sendak's costumes and sets—is not to be missed. 🕐 15 min. 321 Mercer St. ☎ 206/684-7200. www.seattle opera.org. Ticket prices for performances vary.

The Olympic Sculpture Park is operated by the Seattle Art Museum.

Seattle **Film & Theater**

1 Harvard Exit
2 Joe Bar Coffee
3 Egyptian Theatre
4 Paramount Theatre
5 ACT
6 5th Avenue Theatre
7 Cinerama
8 Seattle Repertory Theatre
9 Intiman Theatre

Seattleites spend their long summer days outdoors, but come fall, it's time to head for the theater. So perhaps the rainy winters have played a role in making this an important film and theater town. The monthlong Seattle International Film Festival (☎ 206/633-7151; www.seattlefilm.org), held in May at several venues throughout the city, is the largest film festival in the country and has launched a number of world premieres. The city also boasts several magnificent theaters built in the Roaring Twenties or earlier, as vaudeville houses, playhouses, movie palaces, or clubs. START: **Bus 49 to E. Roy St. and Harvard Ave.**

1 Harvard Exit. Tucked away in an unassuming brick building on a side street in the artsy Capitol Hill neighborhood, this theater specializes in independent and foreign-language films. Built in 1925 as a clubhouse for The Woman's Century Club, it was converted to a movie theater in the '60s. In addition to its cozy fireplace, grand piano, and comfy chairs, the huge lobby houses a 1919 movie projector that was once used to make silent films. Parking can be tricky around here, so leave yourself plenty of time if you come for a show. 🕐 15 min. 807 E. Roy at Harvard. ☎ 206/781-5755. www.landmark theatres.com/Market/Seattle/Harvard ExitTheatre.htm. Free admission to see the lobby.

A detail from the Egyptian Theatre's elaborate lobby art.

2 Joe Bar Coffee. The coffee drinks are great, but here they must share top billing with a menu of light, delectable crepes, both sweet and savory. You can mix and match ingredients to your taste. There may be a line inside this chic, cozy spot, but you can fill the time admiring the work of budding artists—and enjoying CDs of indie rockers. If it's crowded downstairs, try the loft. *810 E. Roy.* ☎ *206/324-0407. $*

3 ★ Egyptian Theatre. Though built in 1915, this former Masonic Temple didn't adopt its Egyptian theme until the '80s, when it became home to the Seattle International Film Festival. Still one of the main SIFF venues, the Egyptian shows classic, foreign, and independent films the rest of the year. You can usually find parking along the street or in one of several nearby lots, or in the Seattle Central Community College garage across the street. 🕐 15 min. 801 E. Pine St. ☎ 206/323-4978.

4 ★★ Paramount Theatre. I have just one complaint about this opulent theater: I often find myself transfixed by the ceiling instead of the stage. Not that the shows aren't riveting. The Broadway series, silent movies, comedy, and diverse range of concerts are first-rate. It's just that the French Renaissance architecture

A detail from the 5th Avenue Theatre's elaborate ceiling.

is so lavish, and the intricate ceiling so intriguing, that the architecture can almost steal the show. Built in 1928 as Seattle's most spectacular theater, the Paramount treated guests to stage shows and silent films, shown to the accompaniment of a custom-made Wurlitzer organ. Not a bit of its former splendor has been lost, a fact often noted by affluent Seattle brides, who make their entrances down the grand staircase in the lobby. At wedding receptions, the theater's sloped seating area converts to a flat hardwood floor for tables and dancing. ⏱ *15 min. 911 Pine St.* ☎ *206/467-5510. www.the paramount.com. Free admission to the lobby.*

⑤ ACT (A Contemporary Theatre). The focus at this nationally recognized theater is on presenting contemporary and new plays, a number of which have gone on to New York. However, one of its most popular performances is the classic *A Christmas Carol.* The audience sits in a semicircle around the central stage. The longest-running show in Seattle, *Late Nite Catechism,*

has kept ACT audiences laughing for more than a decade. The beautiful 1924 terra-cotta building became home to the ACT in 1973. ⏱ *15 min. 700 Union St.* ☎ *206/292-7676.*

⑥ ★★ 5th Avenue Theatre. The 5th was one of the first vaudeville houses built with an Asian design in the 1920s, when all things Eastern were in vogue. Architect Robert Reamer intended the magnificent interior to look like three Imperial Chinese masterpieces: the Forbidden City, the Temple of Heaven, and the Summer Palace. The theater has undergone two transformations since the vaudeville days: first, to a movie palace; then, after a major renovation in the '80s, to a playhouse. Its stage has been graced by stars the likes of Katharine Hepburn, Robert Goulet, and Carol Channing. The 5th hosts more than 100 live performances each year, including touring Broadway musicals and Broadway-bound shows. ⏱ *15 min. 1308 5th Ave.* ☎ *206/625-1418. www.5thavenue.org.*

⑦ ★ Cinerama. Remember the old wraparound cineramic films?

You can still see them at the historic Seattle Cinerama Theatre, one of only three venues in the world that can show the classic three-panel Cinerama films. Once sentenced to be torn down, Cinerama was saved in 1999 by former Microsoft co-founder Paul Allen. And, as you might expect, the renovation was done in high-tech fashion, with a 90-foot-long (27m) louvered screen and cutting-edge acoustics. There's also a smaller screen for contemporary films. ⏱ *15 min. 2100 4th Ave.* ☎ *206/441-3080. www.cinerama. com.*

⑧ Seattle Repertory Theatre.

This Tony Award–winning regional venue has two stages, both housed in a graceful curved building in the northwest corner of Seattle Center. The Rep's offerings tend to be important, beautifully performed literary and artistic productions. ⏱ *15 min. 155 Mercer St.* ☎ *206/443-2210.*

⑨ Intiman Theatre. Specializing

in international drama—both classics

ACT features mostly modern works.

and contemporary plays—this intimate Tony Award–winning regional theater has launched several world premieres. Its shows have delighted Seattle audiences for more than 3 decades. The Intiman is sandwiched between the Seattle Repertory Theatre and the Pacific Northwest Ballet's McCaw Hall. ⏱ *15 min. 201 Mercer St.* ☎ *206/269-1900.*

The Paramount Theatre is not to be missed.

Seattle **for Kids**

1 Seattle Aquarium
2 Seattle Children's Theatre
3 Seattle Center House Food Court
4 Seattle Children's Museum
5 Pacific Science Center
6 Northwest Puppet Center
7 Woodland Park Zoo
8 Green Lake Park

Though Seattle is heavy on young professionals with relatively few kids, it is an unusually child-friendly town. Glaring shopkeepers and condescending waiters are rare. Kids will love the natural beauty of Puget Sound, the mountains, and parks, and there is a wealth of activities to keep youngsters busy any time of the year.
START: **Waterfront Streetcar Line (bus route 99) to Pier 59.**

Experience the beauty of underwater life at the Seattle Aquarium.

① ★★ **Seattle Aquarium.** Children's programs are frequently offered, with stories for tots and crafts for older kids. Most are included with admission; others cost a small additional fee. Check the schedule on the aquarium's website. Kids also love the tidepool exhibit, where they can get their hands on anemones and sea stars. ⏱ *2 hr. 1483 Alaskan Way on Pier 59.* ☎ *206/ 386-4300. www.seattleaquarium. org. Admission $15 adults, $10 ages 4–12. Daily 9:30am–5pm. See p 96.*

② ★★★ **Seattle Children's Theatre.** This is theater that adults can enjoy as much as their offspring. Professional actors perform plays based on beloved classic and contemporary books and movies. The sets are clever, the costumes ingenious, and the acting first-rate. The season runs September through June, with performances

Friday through Sunday afternoons and evenings. You can order an intermission snack when you arrive

Even adults will be entertained by the inventive performances at the Seattle Children's Theatre.

at the children's theater, and it will be ready and waiting for your child during the break. Otherwise, expect to stand in line during the entire intermission when you could be going down the hall to check out the gift area, which is stocked with books and unusual items that relate to the show. Afterward, the actors line up to chat with kids and give autographs. Stop in to pick up tickets for a post-tour show. *201 Thomas St., at Seattle Center.* ☎ *206/441-3322. www.sct.org. Ticket prices vary.*

3 **Seattle Center House Food Court.** You'll find lots of quick and tasty options here, from Thai noodles to fish and chips. Of course, there are plenty of treats as well, from sugar-dusted beignets to homemade taffy. The perfect "grown-up" outing for kids is dinner at the Seattle Center House food court, followed by a play at the Seattle Children's Theatre. *305 Harrison St.* ☎ *206/684-7200. $.*

4 ★ **Seattle Children's Museum.** Check the website for the current special exhibit. Most are geared toward the 6-and-under set, but children up to 10 will enjoy the hands-on science section and Imagination Studio, where they can work on a variety of art projects. Make that an early stop, in case paint needs to dry, then pick up the finished product on your way out. ⏱ *90 min. 305 Harrison St.* ☎ *206/441-1768. www.thechildrens museum.org. Admission $7.50 for adults & children, free for kids under age 1. Mon–Fri 10am–5pm; Sat–Sun 10am–6pm. See p 107.*

5 ★★ **Pacific Science Center.** In addition to the myriad exhibits for older kids, the center has a crawl-and-climb area, including a

treehouse, for tinier tots. They can even play in the water in a "stream" set up at table height. Smocks are available. Also, check for special exhibits on your way in; these range from amazing bubble demonstrations to live animal shows. ⏱ *2 hr. 200 2nd Ave. N.* ☎ *206/443-2844. www.pacsci.org. Admission $11 adults, $9.50 seniors, $8 ages 6–12, $6 ages 3–5. IMAX $8–$11 adults, $7.50–$9.50 seniors, $7–$8.50 ages 6–12, $6 ages 3–5; discounts available for combination passes. Mon–Fri 10am–5pm; Sat–Sun 10am–6pm. See p 108.*

6 ★★ **Northwest Puppet Center.** The Carter Family Marionettes, a local multi-generational family of puppeteers, present high-quality performances geared toward children of various ages. The artistry is remarkable, and the genial Carters bring in puppeteers from around the world, using every kind of puppet imaginable. The stories are often based on books or folk tales. Don't leave right after the

Little ones will be thrilled to be let loose in the interactive Seattle Children's Museum.

The Pacific Science Center.

show, because puppets are often brought out on stage for children to come up and touch. *9123 15th Ave. NE.* ☎ *206/523-2579. www.nw puppet.org. Tickets $11 adults, $9 seniors, $8.50 children. Public shows are on weekend afternoons.*

⑦ ★★★ Woodland Park Zoo. One of the first zoos to move animals out of cages and into more natural habitats, Woodland Park has won awards for several exhibits, including the primate area and the African Savanna. The Komodo dragons and the nocturnal exhibit, full of bats and other nighttime creatures, are big draws for kids. The zoo's latest addition is Zoomazium, an indoor play area where kids 8 and under can explore nature, listen to stories, and generally burn off energy. Special programs are

offered for toddlers in the morning and school-age children in the afternoon. The zoo also recently added a beautiful 1918 carousel; rides cost $2. ⏱ *2 hr. 750 N. 50th St.* ☎ *206/ 684-4800. www.zoo.org. Admission May–Sept $15 ages 13–64, $10 ages 3–12; Oct–Apr $11 ages 13–64, $8 ages 3–12. May–Sept daily 9:30am– 6pm; Oct–Apr daily 9:30am–4pm.*

⑧ Green Lake Park. Seattle's favorite place to walk, the 2.8-mile (4.5km) path around lovely Green Lake draws moms with strollers, joggers, dog-walkers, bicyclists, and nature-lovers. An indoor warm-water pool (☎ 206/684-4961) offers family, public, and lap swimming. Tots can splash away in an unusually large outdoor wading pool, open daily 11am to 8pm from mid-June to Labor Day. I liked to take my daughter to the playground here when she was younger, because it's divided into separate areas for toddlers and their rowdier older siblings. *7201 E Green Lake Dr. N.* ☎ *206/684-4075. www.seattle.gov/parks. Open 24 hr.*

The Woodland Park Zoo is famous for its tigers, among other things.

Caffeinated Seattle

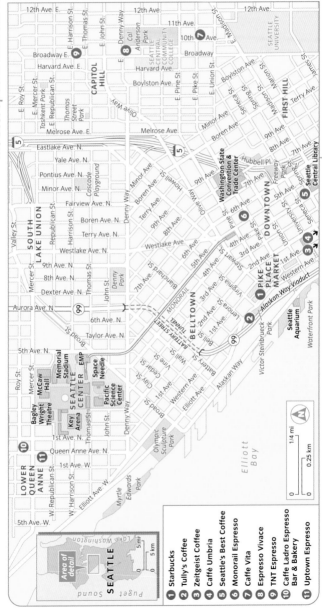

1 Starbucks
2 Tully's Coffee
3 Zeitgeist Coffee
4 Caffé Umbria
5 Seattle's Best Coffee
6 Monorail Espresso
7 Caffe Vita
8 Espresso Vivace
9 TNT Espresso
10 Caffe Ladro Espresso Bar & Bakery
11 Uptown Espresso

Even inveterate tea-drinkers like myself can't help but get caught up in the coffee frenzy that permeates Seattle. Pumpkin-spice lattes, peppermint mochas, white-chocolate lattes with raspberry, caramel macchiatos—who could resist their favorite flavors blended tastefully with the drug that keeps Seattleites going through the drizzle? Purists may opt for espresso or Americanos. If you just don't like coffee, try a chai tea latte. There's no coffee in it, just creamy, delightfully spiced tea that makes the world seem warm and cozy. In the summer, order your favorite drink served over ice. Don't worry about being picky; the person in line ahead of you is likely to demand a double short half-caff extra-hot soy no-foam latte. Watch the barista's face—he or she won't miss a beat. START: **Bus 10, 12, or 99 to Pike Place Market.**

1 ★ **Starbucks.** You must begin, of course, where Seattle's coffee culture itself really began back in 1971. The very first Starbucks, at Pike Place Market, still features the chain's original mascot, the topless mermaid with a double fish tail, which has been toned down over the years in other locations. Many coffee-lovers gripe that Starbucks are ubiquitous; others think the beans taste burned. For me, their flavored drinks are hard to beat and consistently good from store to store. *The original: 1912 Pike Place.* ☎ 206/448-8762.

2 ★ kids **Tully's Coffee.** With shops in several western states— including a number in Seattle—

Zeitgeist offers an urbane oasis from busy city life.

Love them or hate them, this is the site where the Starbucks phenomenon began.

Tully's still roasts its coffee painstakingly, in small batches in antique roasters. The stores are friendly and welcoming, the drinks and baked goods terrific, and they usually have tables where kids can read and draw while the grown-ups sit by the fireplace and chat. My favorite is the one near Pike Place Market (2001 Western Ave #110A; ☎ 206/443-1915). *The original: 1401 4th Ave.* ☎ 206/625-0600.

3 ★★ **Zeitgeist.** This spacious, hip European-style coffeehouse serves up film screenings and rotating works by up-and-coming artists

A Star(bucks) Is Born

In 1971, a roasting house named Starbucks, after the first mate in *Moby-Dick*, opened in Pike Place Market. It was a successful local coffeehouse, but all of that changed after now-CEO Howard Schultz joined the company in the early 1980s. A trip to Italy convinced him that scrumptious espresso and cappuccino drinks would be a big hit. He was right, and coffee culture exploded. Soon, Seattleites became grumpy if they were forced to walk more than a block for a latte. By the 1990s, Starbucks was opening a new store somewhere on the globe every day; it now opens seven a day.

along with its popular Italian beans, illy Caffe. *See p 53,* 🔟.

④ ★★ **Caffe Umbria.** The Bizzarri family has been roasting beans since current owner Emanuele's grandfather Ornello opened his first shop in Perugia, Italy. Five blends are available, including fair-trade beans. Umbria's Italian-style coffee is served by many demanding establishments, including the Bellagio Hotel and Resort in Las Vegas. You can enjoy a heavenly extra-foamy cappuccino right here in Pioneer Square. *See p 52,* 7️⃣.

⑤ **Seattle's Best Coffee.** When you're the biggest coffee chain in the world and you have a heavy-hitting competitor, what do you do? Buy it, of course. Which is just what Starbucks did a few years ago with Seattle's Best Coffee, a company that was also an early player on the local coffee scene. But SBCs are still allowed to serve their own coffee blends. The chain got its name many years ago, after it won a contest by a Seattle restaurant for the best cuppa joe in town. The stores have comfy chairs and ambience that make

Coffee has become a major part of Seattle's social scene.

you feel right at home. *Downtown: 1100 4th Ave.* ☎ *206/623-0104. Pike Place Market: 1530 Post Alley.* ☎ *206/467-7700.*

⑥ ★ **Monorail Espresso.** Back in 1980, even before Starbucks began selling coffee drinks at its original store, Chuck Beek came up with the idea of running a little espresso cart in Seattle. He peddled his wares underneath the monorail track. Fifteen years later, with a greatly expanded coffee menu, he opened a permanent shop a few blocks away. It's still some of the best coffee in the city, and the prices are more reasonable than most. Try the vanilla latte, yum. *520 Pike St. (at 5th).* ☎ *206/625-0449.*

⑦ ★ **Caffe Vita.** This roastery also claims many devotees who swear by its beans and blends from around the world. Vita forms relationships with coffee growers in Africa, Indonesia, and the Americas, and offers a wide variety of tastes. *Capitol Hill: 1005 E. Pike St.* ☎ *206/709-4440. Queen Anne: 813 5th Ave. N.* ☎ *206/285-9662.*

Is it really Seattle's best? After this tour, you'll be able to make an educated decision.

8 ★★ **Espresso Vivace.** David Schomer's slow-roasting process is designed to produce a sweet caramel flavor, and the roasting is stopped early to keep the oils in and prevent a burned flavor. For many coffee aficionados, this is as good as it gets. Vivace roasts only two varieties: a latte blend (with a decaffeinated version) and an espresso blend. *Capitol Hill cafe location: 901 E. Denny Way.* ☎ *206/860-5869. Capitol Hill Stand: 321 Broadway Ave. E.*

9 ★ **TNT Espresso.** This small, friendly Capitol Hill stand serves Zoka coffee, which is roasted in Seattle using beans from around the globe, including an organic chocolaty fair-trade blend of beans from Java and Yemen. Zoka's Paladino blend is especially sweet and nutty, and is a favorite of many baristas at competitions. *328 Broadway Ave E.* ☎ *206/323-9151.*

10 **Caffe Ladro Espresso Bar & Bakery.** Serving only organic, fair-trade, shade-grown coffee, Caffe Ladro has about a dozen locations around metro Seattle. The shops are all urban-hip, with delicious quiche and baked goods. Try a Medici latte, flavored with orange peel.

600 Queen Anne Ave. N. ☎ *206/ 282-1549. Downtown: 801 Pine St.* ☎ *206/405-1950.*

11 ★ **Uptown Espresso.** This is a serious coffee shop, with rough wood tables occupied by quietly chatting friends and furiously typing computer-users. Lattes come topped with a layer of Uptown's heavenly Velvet Foam. *With locations all over town: 525 Queen Anne Ave N.* ☎ *206/285-3757. Belltown: 2504 4th Ave.* ☎ *206/ 441-1084.*

The drinks at Espresso Vivace look like works of art.

42

Seattle Architecture & Design

The Best Special-Interest Tours

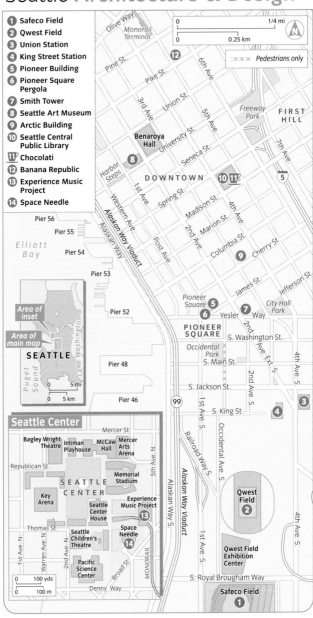

1. Safeco Field
2. Qwest Field
3. Union Station
4. King Street Station
5. Pioneer Building
6. Pioneer Square Pergola
7. Smith Tower
8. Seattle Art Museum
9. Arctic Building
10. Seattle Central Public Library
11. Chocolati
12. Banana Republic
13. Experience Music Project
14. Space Needle

Though a city this young may not have the widest range of architectural styles, there are many historic gems to be found here, and Seattleites have put a great deal of cash into preserving their colorful past. Most of the renovations have been undertaken with care, and it is delightful to see the modern uses to which these old buildings have been put, with all due respect paid to their histories. But architecture here is also moving forward. The city's rapid growth and penchant for adventure has attracted world-renowned architects, who have designed a number of cutting-edge buildings. START: **Bus 15, 18, 21, 22, or 56 to Safeco Field.**

1 ★ kids **Safeco Field.** The Seattle Mariners' stadium opened in 1999 after the team demanded a new facility to replace the not-so-old but leaky Kingdome. It was built amid even more controversy than usual in Seattle, but has won over most hearts, at least in part because it keeps the rain off while letting the fresh air in. It has one of the few retractable stadium coverings in the country, and the only one that doesn't fully enclose the field. On a perfect sunny day when the roof is open, baseball doesn't get better than this. If you can't make it to a game, take the hour-long tour. ⏱ 1 hr. 1250 1st Ave. S. ☎ 206/346-4287. www.mariners.mlb.com. Ticket prices for games vary. Tour $8 adults, $7 seniors, $6 ages 3–12, free for children under 3.

Check out a baseball game at the ultra-modern Safeco Field.

2 ★ **Qwest Field.** The Mariners weren't the only Seattle sports team to demand a new stadium—

the Seahawks also insisted on moving out of the ill-fated Kingdome. So it was destroyed in a fantastic implosion and replaced by Qwest Field. The new facility's graceful double-arched roof, studded with glowing

The tour of Qwest Field gives a behind-the-scenes look at the stadium.

A totem pole guards the entry to the Pioneer Building.

blue lights that you'll spot as you fly into the city or drive along I-5, has become a treasured part of the city's skyline. The roof also over-hangs most of the bleachers, keeping about 70 percent of the fans dry. The field is open-air, and so is the north end, which allows drop-dead views of downtown. If you want to taste the luxury suite experience without the expense, take a tour—they're offered all year long. ⏲ *90 min. 800 Occidental Ave S.* ☎ *206/381-7555. www.qwestfield.com. Tours $7 adults, $5 seniors & ages 4–12. Sept 1–May 31 Fri–Sat 12:30pm & 2:30pm; June 1–Aug 31 daily 12:30pm & 2:30pm.*

❸ ★ **Union Station.** Opened in 1911, this was a transcontinental train station for 60 years. Sadly, the place was abandoned in 1971 and the vast Beaux Arts building then sat deteriorating until Microsoft billion-aire Paul Allen and his deep pockets came to the rescue. Now it serves as the headquarters for Sound Transit, a regional commuter train. Its

spectacular hall, which features a beautifully lighted barrel-vaulted ceil-ing, is rented out for weddings and other grand occasions, and it's easy to see why. In the daytime, natural light pours in through an enormous semi-circular window. The elegant architecture is worth an admiring look. ⏲ *15 min. 401 S. Jackson St.* ☎ *206/682-7275. Free admission.*

❹ **King Street Station.** This bustling Amtrak and Sound Transit commuter station was built in 1906 for the Great Northern Railway and Northern Pacific Railway. It has not been fully restored to its former glory, though efforts to do so are under way. Much of the renovating will require undoing damage done in the 1960s, when elaborate, high ceil-ings and other ornate features were covered up. But the stunning entry hall, dubbed the Compass Room because of the marble-tiled direc-tional points marked on the floor, has been restored and is worth a quick peek. The station's clock tower, once the tallest structure in Seattle, is a stately local landmark. ⏲ *15 min. 303 S. Jackson St.* ☎ *206/382-4125. Free admission. Mon–Fri 6am–7pm; Sat–Sun 6am–5pm.*

❺ **Pioneer Building.** This ele-gant, Romanesque-style structure, hurriedly built right after the Great Fire, was named the "finest building west of Chicago" by the American Institute of Architects when it was completed in 1892. Underground Tour offers a fascinating look at the building and at Seattle's colorful history, if you have the time (tours are 90 min.). ⏲ *15 min. 1st Ave. & Yesler Way. Underground Tour, 610 1st Ave. #200.* ☎ *206/682-4646. www.undergroundtour.com. $14 adults, $7 children 7–12. Tours offered daily, throughout the day. See p 51.*

❻ ★ **Pioneer Square Pergola.** You wouldn't know it today, but

Seattle's eye-catching iron-and-glass pergola (that's a type of arbor, for those not familiar with the term) gained its fame for what once lay beneath: elegant public restrooms made of marble and bronze, widely considered the most luxurious in the world when they opened in 1910. People would enter the restrooms on stairways leading from the pergola. It was a project in keeping with Seattle's traditional egalitarian ethics. The "comfort stations" have long since been closed, and the graceful Victorian pergola itself was crushed by a veering truck in 2001. Fortunately, it was restored the next year with as much of the original materials as possible. ⏱ *15 min. 1st Ave. & Yesler Way.*

⑦ **Smith Tower.** The tallest building west of the Mississippi when it was built in 1914, this 42-story neo-classical office building is a grand old lady, worth a visit if only for a ride in its brass-caged elevators. They're the last manually operated ones on the West Coast. The elaborate Chinese Room, with its carved blackwood furniture, is on the 35th floor, as is the observation deck, and both are open to the public. The view, which takes in everything from Safeco Field to Mt. Rainier (at least on a clear day) is spectacular. ⏱ *30 min. 506 2nd Ave.* ☎ *206/622-4004. www.smithtower.com. Observation deck admission $7.50 adults, $5 kids 6–12, free for children under 6. Apr–Oct daily 10am–sunset; Nov–Mar weekends only 10am–3:30pm, except during private events, so check the schedule in advance.*

⑧ **★★★ Seattle Art Museum.** Built in a decade that saw a flurry of cultural projects in Seattle, this gem of a museum was designed by Pritzker Prize–winner Robert Venturi. The facility opened in this new location in 1991, after spending its first 60 years in an Art Deco building in Volunteer Park that now houses the Seattle Asian Art Museum. Fifteen years later, the museum was again bursting at the seams, and a large expansion by Brad Cloepfil of Allied Works Architecture was finished in 2007. The outside of the building—the upper 12 floors of which house the main offices of Washington Mutual—is short of spectacular, but the harmonious blending of old and new is impressive. The "wow" factor was reserved for the lovely interior, where exhibit

After being crushed by a truck in 2001, the Pioneer Square Peragola is back to its former glory.

Say hello to the walruses who adorn the Arctic Building.

spaces have doubled in size, prompting donations of 1,000 new pieces of art. ⏱ *1 hr. 1300 1st Ave.* ☎ *206/654-3100. www.seattleart museum.org. Admission $13 adults, $10 seniors over 62, $7 students & kids 13–17, free for kids 12 & under. Tues–Sun 10am–5pm; Thurs–Fri 10am–9pm. See p 65.*

⑨ Arctic Building. Fondly dubbed the "Walrus Building," this eight-story Art Deco structure was once an exclusive club for the relatively few gold miners who struck it rich in the Yukon. In homage to the land where those riches were made, the building featured Alaskan marble hallways and a row of sculpted walrus heads around the third floor of the colorful terra-cotta exterior. Members could indulge in just about everything here, from formal teas to bowling. The city of Seattle sold the building in 2005 to investors who transformed it into the Arctic Club Hotel, which features period decor.

⏱ *15 min. 700 3rd Ave.* ☎ *206/340-0340. www.articclubhotel.com. Free admission to the lobby. See p 147.*

⑩ ★★★ kids Seattle Central Public Library. The most talked-about design in Seattle—since the Experience Music Project museum, at least—is the $165 million central public library, an avant-garde showpiece by Dutch architect Rem Koolhaas. This is not your average library. Tourists from around the world have been coming specifically to see this building since its 2004 opening. Outside, its odd, asymmetrical glass and steel angles jut powerfully over the sidewalk. Inside, patrons walk up a spiraling floor that gradually leads to the top floor. Elevators and electric-hued escalators are another option. On your way up, stunning views of the surrounding downtown buildings can be seen through the netlike steel structure. ⏱ *30 min. 1000 4th Ave.* ☎ *206/386-4636. www.spl.org. Free admission. Mon–Thurs 10am–8pm; Fri–Sat 10am–6pm; Sun noon–6pm.*

⑪ Chocolati. Need a quick pick-me-up after all of your architectural exploring? You'll find it at the espresso stand inside Seattle Central Public Library. A limited

Wooden carvings overlook Smith Tower's old-fashioned elevators.

selection of baked goods is available, or warm up with a Peppermint Patty hot chocolate. *1000 4th Ave.* ☎ *206/386-4636. $.*

⓬ **Banana Republic.** Yes, it's a chain store, but it's a chain store set in a stunning building that once housed the old Coliseum Theatre. It was built in 1916 by renowned Seattle architect B. Marcus Priteca for wealthy local property owner Joseph Gottstein. The Coliseum was one of the first elegant movie palaces, and is unusual in that it was specifically designed to show (then-silent) films at a time when many movie houses were simply renovated stage theaters. Priteca also designed the Pantages chain of theaters, including California's famous one at Hollywood & Vine. After the boom in suburban theaters in the '70s, the Coliseum stood empty until its reinvention as a clothing store. Happily, the original grandeur is preserved, and the white terra-cotta exterior is striking. ⏱ *15 min. 500 Pike St.* ☎ *206/622-2303.*

⓭ ★ **Experience Music Project.** Without question, this is the oddest structure in Seattle. It was built by eccentric Microsoft co-founder Paul Allen, a huge fan of late guitar legend Jimi Hendrix, who

The Seattle Public Library.

was a Seattle native. At ground level the museum looks, well, rather like amorphous blobs of colorful sheet-metal, but from the air, designer Frank Gehry's building is supposed to resemble one of Jimi's famed guitars. The inside, also architecturally interesting, showcases the history of rock 'n' roll, including its roots in soul, jazz, and other genres. There is also a relatively new museum within the museum, the Science Fiction Museum and Hall of Fame. ⏱ *1 hr. 325 5th Ave. N. (at Seattle Center).* ☎ *206/770-2700. www. empsfm.org. Admission $15 adults,*

Heads Up!

One of the best ways to sample the city's architecture is to take one of the many popular walking tours offered by the Seattle Architecture Foundation. They last from 1 to 3 hours and showcase a wide variety of styles and locations, from the Seattle waterfront to the Art Deco district to the Craftsman bungalows north of the city. Check the website (www.seattlearchitecture.org) for dates and times. Most tours cost $10 in advance or $12 for same-day tickets, and most 3-hour walks cost $20, advance sales only.

The Experience Music Project is one of Seattle's most fascinating buildings.

$12 seniors & children 5–17, free for children 4 & under. Daily 10am–5pm.

⑭ ★★★ **kids** **Space Needle.** In typical Seattle fashion, there was much disagreement over what the centerpiece for the 1962 World's Fair should look like and where it should go. The futuristic design

The Space Needle defines the Seattle skyline.

morphed considerably from the original "Needle" sketched out on a paper placemat by a hotel chain president. By the time architect John Graham (designer of Seattle's Northgate, the first shopping mall in the world) and his team came up with something everyone agreed on, the fair was only 1½ years away. Finding a site was even trickier, and was finally accomplished with just 13 months to go. Construction went at breakneck speed, and the last elevator car arrived the day before the fair opened. The Space Needle went on to become the world-renowned symbol for its city, and in 2000 got a very snazzy $20-million face-lift. 🕐 *1 hr. 400 Broad St.* ☎ *206/9052180. www.spaceneedle. com. Observation deck admission $16 adults, $14 seniors, $8 ages 4–13. Sun–Thurs 9am–11pm; Fri–Sat 9am–noon.* See p 107. ●

3 The Best
Neighborhood Walks

Pioneer Square

1 Pioneer Building
2 Pioneer Square Park
3 Merchants Cafe
4 Seattle Mystery Bookshop
5 Smith Tower
6 Waterfall Garden Park
7 Caffè Umbria
8 Glasshouse Studio
9 Klondike Gold Rush International Historical Park
10 Zeitgeist Coffee
11 Elliott Bay Book Company

For a taste of Seattle's quirky past, wander the oddly angled streets of Pioneer Square, where some of the city's finest art galleries are interspersed with shops and restaurants. The charming Victorian brick and stone buildings were slapped up after the Great Fire of 1889 by local fat cats, eager to get back to selling supplies—and services of every kind—to prospectors en route to the Yukon. At night, the district's clubs still spring to life. START: **Bus 15, 16, 18, 21, 22, 56, or 99 to Pioneer Sq.**

1 ★★ **Pioneer Building.** Begin your tour at the very spot where pioneer Henry Yesler built his sawmill in the 1850s, then rebuilt it after the Great Fire of 1889 (p 44). He hired famed architect Elmer Fisher—who designed more than 50 post-fire structures—to create the stylish building. Go inside and check out Doc Maynard's Pub, the Pioneer Square Antique Mall (a labyrinth of shops in the basement), and the entertaining Underground Tour, which gives you the insider account of Seattle's colorful past. This is one of my favorite ways to amuse visitors. 🕐 *90 min. 1st Avenue & Yesler Way. Underground Tour, 610 1st Ave #200.* ☎ *206/682-4646. www.undergroundtour.com. $14 adults, $7 children 7–12. Tours offered daily, throughout the day.*

2 ★ **Pioneer Square Park.** The pergola (p 44), Seattle's most beloved hunk of iron, graces the south end of this triangular park—really more of a courtyard—directly in front of the Pioneer Building. It's popular with tourists, but also with vagrants looking for a bench to while away the day. Though the city has a low crime rate, it's always good to stay alert. Another rebuilt item in the park is a 60-foot (18m) Tlingit totem pole, a replacement for one stolen in 1899 from an Alaskan village by a "Good Will Committee" of leading Seattle citizens. When the pole burned years later,

the city hired the descendants of the original Native American carvers to produce its replacement. 🕐 *15 min. 1st Ave. & Yesler Way.*

3 **Merchants Cafe.** Step back in time at the oldest watering hole in Seattle. Back in the day, prospectors would quaff a brew at the saloon, then head upstairs to the brothel, now converted into apartments. So much gold was dropped here by prospectors on the weekends that it came to be known as the Sunday Bank. Today, you can enjoy lunch, dinner, or a beer in the remodeled restaurant. 🕐 *15 min. 109 Yesler Way.* ☎ *206/935-7625. Daily 11am–2am.*

4 **Seattle Mystery Bookshop.** Whodunit aficionados can spend hours tracking down mystery books, both collectable and current, at this terrific little shop. There are frequent author signings, and if you miss one you like, check with the owner, JB—he keeps a large number of autographed volumes on hand. 🕐 *15 min. 117 Cherry St.* ☎ *206/587-5737. www.seattlemystery.com. Mon–Sat 10am–5pm & Sun noon–5pm.*

Seattle Mystery Bookshop is the perfect place to wile away a few hours.

5 ★ **Smith Tower.** Ride the antique cage elevators up to the 35th floor observation deck of this building for a fabulous view of downtown Seattle and Mt. Rainier, though the building is now dwarfed by more modern 'scrapers. ⏱ *30 min. 506 2nd Ave.* ☎ *206/622-4004. www.smithtower.com. Observation deck admission $7.50 adults, $5 kids 6–12, free for children under 6. Apr–Oct daily 10am–sunset; Nov–Mar weekends only 10am–3:30pm, except during private events, so check the schedule in advance. See p 45.*

6 ★★ **Waterfall Garden Park.** This little-known oasis is my favorite place to hang out with a latte. Just follow the sound of the crash of water tumbling 22 feet (7m) down a wall of boulders—it delightfully drowns out the urban bustle. Waterfall Garden Park is a two-level gem of a spot, built in honor of United Parcel Service employees. At lunchtime, office workers escape the concrete and lunch amid its trees and flowers. ⏱ *15 min. 219 2nd Ave. S.*

7 **Caffe Umbria.** OK, so the Emerald City is not exactly known for its hot weather, but that's never kept a Seattleite from indulging in a frozen treat. A favorite is the sinfully creamy gelato at Caffe Umbria. I highly

recommend the cappuccino and pistachio flavors. Sit at the window bar, gazing out at the passersby ogling the Occidental Park art galleries. If you're hungry, the panini sandwiches and croissants are fresh and delicious. *320 Occidental Ave. S.* ☎ *206/624-5847. $.*

8 ★★ **kids Glasshouse Studio.** Seattle is home to some of the world's finest glass artists—Dale Chihuly, famed for his outrageously colorful, fanciful works, has a studio on Lake Union. In Pioneer Square, you can watch artists at work in Seattle's oldest glassblowing studio as they shape glowing globs of color into the most amazing things of beauty. You can buy their vases, figurines, chandeliers, and jewelry in the adjacent shop. ⏱ *30 min. 311 Occidental Ave. S.* ☎ *206/682-9939. www.glasshouse-studio.com. Mon–Sat 10am–5pm; Sun 11am–4pm.*

9 ★ **kids Klondike Gold Rush International Historical Park.** In 1897 and 1898, 120,000 fortune-hunters stampeded north to Canada's Yukon Territory, where gold had recently been found. Many of them passed through Seattle, and the impact on the city was enormous. This park tells the story of the

Waterfall Garden Park is one of Seattle's best-kept secrets.

Watch artisans at work at the Glasshouse Studio.

Klondike Gold Rush with great attention to detail (fun fact: 1 in 10 of those headed for the gold fields were women). *1 hr. 319 2nd Ave. S.* ☎ *206/220-4240. www.nps.gov/klse. Free admission. Daily 9am–5pm. See p 22.*

🔟 Drop by **Zeitgeist Coffee** for a muffuletta sandwich and espresso, then enjoy people-watching or discussing world events. If the conversation turns contentious, a world globe and a monster-size dictionary are on hand to help resolve matters. *171 S. Jackson St.* ☎ *206/583-0497. $.*

⓫ ★★★ **kids Elliott Bay Book Company.** Seattleites love their books, and this is the city's favorite bookstore. Be warned—it's easy to get lost here, poking around the nooks and crannies for hours. Which is perfectly fine with management— they never rush you. Should you get hungry or need a caffeine fix, wander downstairs to the cafe, where you can borrow a book from the shelves lining the walls and read while you sip. Or take in one of the frequent author readings. 🕐 *30 min. 101 S. Main St.* ☎ *206/624-6600. www. elliottbaybook.com. Mon–Sat 9:30am–10pm; Sun 11am–7pm.*

First Thursday Gallery Walk

This monthly event is great fun, and a terrific way to catch all the latest exhibits. Best of all, it's free. Wildly popular with local art-lovers and those who want to rub shoulders with artistes, First Thursday showcases the Pioneer Square area's eclectic array of avant-garde galleries. Skip that big dinner before you come, because many of the galleries serve wine and cheese. The best new artists and exhibits are featured, and the art ranges from paintings to sculptures to blown glass. The Seattle Art Museum also opens its doors for free. It all starts at Main Street and Occidental, in Occidental Park. If you really want to go in style, hire one of the horse-drawn carriages circling the area. From 6 to 8pm the first Thursday of every month except January.

Pike Place Market

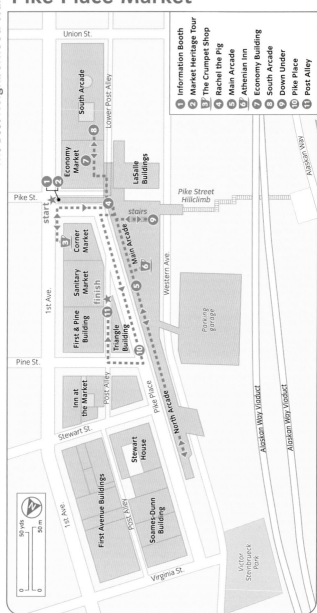

1 Information Booth
2 Market Heritage Tour
3 The Crumpet Shop
4 Rachel the Pig
5 Main Arcade
6 Athenian Inn
7 Economy Building
8 South Arcade
9 Down Under
10 Pike Place
11 Post Alley

Always buzzing with tourists, savvy locals, and finicky restaurateurs, Pike Place Market is the soul of Seattle. Kids love the street performers and the "flying" fish; adults are mesmerized by the mind-boggling variety of shops, food, and entertainment. You can find just about anything you want here, from salted herring to $4,000-a-pound Piemontese truffles to handmade mandolins. It's a wonderful place to spend the day—or two. Plus, it's the only neighborhood in town where jaywalking won't get you a ticket!

START: **Bus 11, 12, 15, 18, 21, 22, 49, or 56 to Pike Place Market.**

1 Information Booth. Make this your first stop—not just to arm yourself with a market newspaper and map, but to check out the half-price tickets available for shows in town that day. You'll find plenty to choose from, ranging from Seattle Children's Theatre productions to Broadway shows. Discounted tickets are also available here for the popular Argosy Cruises of the harbor and Seattle's lakes and locks. *Pike St. & 1st Ave.* ☎ *206/324-2744 (recording only).*

2 Market Heritage Tour. You can pick up some great insider tips on shopping the market on this hour-long jaunt, which leaves from

Start your visit to Pike Place Market at the Information Booth.

the Information Booth. You'll find out how the market came to be in 1907, and how it almost came not to be in the 1970s. Happily, Seattleites decided they couldn't bear to see it demolished and turned into parking garages and office buildings. ⏱ *1 hr.* ☎ *206/774-5249. $10 for adults, $6 for seniors & children under 18. Reserve 24 hr. in advance for weekday tours, by 4pm Fri for Sat. Tours start at 11am Wed–Fri & 9:30am Sat.*

3 ★ The Crumpet Shop. As a tea fanatic in a java town, I especially appreciate this charming British spot, which always has several varieties of tasty global teas brewed up, with free refills. Of course, there are also the mouth-watering crumpets, baked fresh daily. Crumpet purists can get one with just marmalade, but I love them with smoked salmon, cream cheese, and cucumber. If you get there early, you can watch the bakers at work. *1503 1st Ave.* ☎ *206/682-1598. $.*

4 kids Rachel the Pig. Seattle's beloved bronze porker stands just under the famous neon "Public Market Center" sign and clock. I like to drop a coin or two in the piggybank to help support the Market Foundation's charities, which were started in the 1970s. The civic-minded folks who saved the Market decided the revival should include social services, including low-income apartments for

Spirit of the Market

Tales abound of ghosts and ghouls wandering among the narrow halls, stairwells, dusty corners, and nooks and crannies of Pike Place Market, looking for closure—or at least their old haunts. So many ghosts have been reported by workers and visitors to the Market that a few even have names—like Jacob, supposedly a horse groom in real life, back in the days when the Market had stables. Now he's fabled to haunt the Down Under, where he reportedly mixes up the bead colors at the Bead Zone shop. Then there's Frank, who supposedly introduces himself to guests at the Alibi Room nightclub before fading away. And more than one ghost has been reported hanging around Kell's Irish Pub on Post Alley, the former site of a mortuary. The Market's colorful history includes brothels, orphans who worked for pennies, a deadly flu epidemic, and the aforementioned mortuary. It all adds up to fertile ground for spirits. Even if you don't believe in them, you'll enjoy taking a ghost tour of the Market. Mercedes Yaeger, whose father started the tours a quarter-century ago, offers these hour-long walks which meet at 6pm Fridays and Saturdays in front of Rachel the Pig. Tickets cost $15; call ☎ 206/322-1218 for information or reservations, or order tickets online (www.seattleghost.com).

seniors. Rachel, who has quite a cult following, inspired Pigs on Parade, an occasional summertime event in which 100 fiberglass pigs of various whimsical designs—such as a cubist "Pigasso" and another one covered with espresso beans—are placed throughout the city, then auctioned off to benefit the foundation. A few

Go ahead, climb up on Rachel for a photo.

years ago, it was "Ponies on Parade." Spotting them scattered around town is like a "Where's Waldo" puzzle. *Pike Place & Pike St.*

⑤ ★★ kids Main Arcade. Get ready for sensory overload! The most tender asparagus, freshest daffodils, richest sockeye salmon, and most unusual Northwest crafts can be found here. Start right behind Rachel the Pig and elbow your way—no easy task in the summertime—through the North Arcade. Everything sold here is required to be grown, caught, or created locally. From the world-famous fish-throwers at Pike Place Fish Market to the tulip-growers from the Skagit Valley, the North Arcade is alive with scents, sounds, and exuberant colors. Salad greens with edible flowers? Chocolate pasta? Pepper jelly? You'll find it here. I always try the tasty free samples at Sosio's Fruit & Produce, and stop for a

Be sure to dodge the flying fish as you head through the Fish Market.

complimentary cup of specially blended Market Spice Tea at Market Spice, which has been in the market since 1911. But don't stuff yourself, because there are plenty of fabulous places to eat here (see "Dining at the Market," below). Head to the back of the shop and look for the carafe. On the north end of the Main Arcade, you'll find the handmade-craft booths. Here you can buy anything from clay ocarinas to watercolor paintings of umbrellas. ⏱ *90 min. Mon–Sat 10am–6pm; Sun 11am–5pm.*

6⃝ Athenian Inn. Tucked off the Main Arcade, this is a favorite hangout of longtime Seattleites, and also of many tourists who remember it from *Sleepless in Seattle.* You can get all-day breakfast here, or seafood straight from the Market. It's a dark, homey kind of place with a long bar. You might think the view is great downstairs, but insist on the upper floor, with its panoramic views of Puget Sound. *1517 Pike Place #1517.* ☎ *206/624-7166. $$.*

7⃝ Economy Building. On the corner of this building, beside the Information Booth, is **First and Pike News,** where the shelves groan under the weight of newspapers from around the world and magazines of every ilk. If you're from another big city, you're likely to find your hometown paper here. **DeLaurenti's Specialty Food Market** is a favorite spot for Seattleites to buy wine, cheese, and olive oil. It also has a terrific deli. What I like best is being able to pick the brains of the knowledgeable staff, who have never steered me wrong in their advice on buying vino. On your way to the Economy Atrium, you'll pass by the nut, crepe, and doughnut kiosks. It's fun to stop and play at **The Great Wind-Up,** which specializes in (what else?) wind-up toys. I can never resist the try-out table, which is generally monopolized by adults with big, goofy grins on their faces. Present company excepted. And chili-lovers won't want to miss the award-winning **World Class Chili.** ⏱ *30 min.*

One of many street performers at the market.

Dining at the Market

Dining options at Pike Place Market range from booths of sausage, noodles, and pastries to first-rate restaurants like Place Pigalle, perched over the water and serving mussels to die for. For a budget lunch, I like to pick up sandwiches in the market, then head toward the water from Rachel the Pig, where there's a tucked-away indoor sitting area with the same panoramic view of the Sound that you'll get in the high-end restaurants.

8 South Arcade. The Economy Building opens onto a newer row of shops and restaurants, including **Pike Pub & Brewery,** one of the area's many excellent microbreweries. **Northwest Tribal Art** is a great place to find colorful masks, totem poles, soapstone figurines, and silver jewelry crafted by local Native Americans. If you're there for any significant amount of time, you're likely to see one of the artists come in with his or her latest wares. On the other hand, if it's a T-shirt or other touristy souvenir

Pike Place Market features farm fresh fruit and veggies from all over the Northwest.

You're sure to find the perfect souvenir at one of the many shops Down Under.

you're after, stop in at **The Best of Seattle.** 🕐 *30 min.*

9 ★ Down Under. Pike Place Market is perched on the top of a hillside, with a labyrinth of eclectic stores sprawling beneath the Main Arcade. It's worth venturing down the staircase to explore them. The shops are jammed with gems, books, ethnic clothing, and jewelry, and there's even an old-fashioned barbershop. A variety of craft stores sell unusual items, including **Afghani Crafts** women's clothing; **Hands of the World,** featuring folk art mainly from developing nations; and **Polish Pottery Place,** where beautifully detailed items are made by a handful of families who've been at it for generations. 🕐 *30 min.*

10 ★★ Pike Place. Once you've jostled your way through the market and out into the fresh air (or drizzle), you're still not done. A brick street runs between the Main Arcade and several facing blocks of shops, food stands, restaurants, and yet more

Stop by First and Pike News (p 57) and see what they have in stock.

produce. I always get a chuckle over the "Big Ass Grapes" sold at the corner shop, but I must admit they're appropriately named. This area is just as lively as the inside Market, with street performers entertaining the crowds. Someone could very well be tickling the ivories of a full-size piano on a street corner. The variety of ethnic food stands are great places to grab a snack, and they make clear what an international city Seattle has become. Try the steamed-pork humbow and red bean sesame balls at **Mee Sum Pastries.** Or, for more substantial fare, **Piroshky Piroshky** serves an array of delicious savory and sweet pastries. I usually order the potato and mushroom, with a marzipan piroshky for dessert. Then stop in at the original **Starbucks** for a latte to wash it all down (p 39). 🕐 *30 min.*

⓫ **Post Alley.** Hike east up the hill a block and you'll find yourself on a charming, winding street where the din is lower but the shops and cafes still delightful. **Perennial Tearoom** is nirvana, as far as I'm concerned. It's a lovely place to stop for a spot of tea, then pick out a few varieties

from the wall of teas to take home for later. The shop stocks teas from around the world, as well as teapots and other tea-related merchandise. A block farther south on Post, you can find classy souvenirs—no kidding—at **Made in Washington.** 🕐 *30 min.*

Post Alley is the perfect spot to escape the hubbub of Pike Place Market.

Downtown

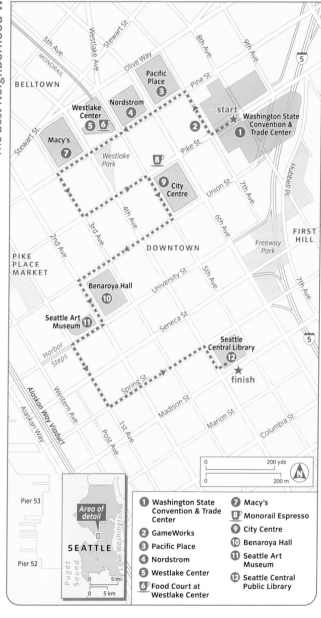

1. Washington State Convention & Trade Center
2. GameWorks
3. Pacific Place
4. Nordstrom
5. Westlake Center
6. Food Court at Westlake Center
7. Macy's
8. Monorail Espresso
9. City Centre
10. Benaroya Hall
11. Seattle Art Museum
12. Seattle Central Public Library

Reinvented in the late '90s, Seattle's downtown core is a world-class destination, bustling with shoppers and gawkers from all over the globe. It's hard to believe this neighborhood was anything but booming in the early 1990s. Even the legendary Frederick & Nelson's department store had shut its doors. But then came the dotcom millionaires, riding to the rescue right on the heels of the grunge rock era, which had already focused the world's attention on the Emerald City. Downtown livened up pretty quickly. Nordstrom, which had started as a humble shoe store way back in 1901, expanded into the old Frederick & Nelson's building; the city's convention center underwent a major expansion; the former Coliseum Theatre was saved and reincarnated as a Banana Republic; and the glitzy Pacific Place mall brought high-end retailers (you can shop at both Tiffany and Cartier here) to town. Today, Seattle's downtown is vibrant, colorful, and one of the most walkable in the country. But if you're loaded down with packages, why not hop on a metro bus? They're free in the downtown area. START: **Bus 10, 11, 12, 43, or 49 to the Washington State Convention & Trade Center.**

❶ **Washington State Convention & Trade Center.** Space was an issue when Seattle's convention center was built in 1988, and it was solved with a unique freeway-straddling design. Look up if you're driving on I-5 and you'll see the center's greenery draping along the overpass. Just a few years later, when the city's economy began to skyrocket, it became clear that the convention center needed yet more elbow room. The problem? There was nowhere to expand, except across Pike Street. So that's just where the other half went in 2001, connected to the original building by an enormous glass skybridge. Enter on the south side of Pike Avenue, and ride up the multiple escalators to check out the ever-changing local art exhibits. If it's raining, you can hang out in the underground concourse, which starts at the convention center, winds under the Seattle Hilton and past shops, cafes, and historical exhibits, and comes out at 5th Avenue Theatre and the Rainier Square Shopping Center. 🕐 *15 min.*

800 Convention Place. ☎ *206/447-5000. www.wsctc.com. Daily 6am–10pm.*

❷ kids **GameWorks.** This 30,000-square-foot (2,700 sq. m) virtual-entertainment center—dreamed up, in part, by Steven Spielberg—was the world's first GameWorks. It is way too loud for my ears, but for kids (including many of the grown-up variety) it's a

Get your one-stop shopping done at Pacific Place (p 62).

The nationwide Nordstrom chain got its start in Seattle.

paradise of futuristic fun and games. You can stay all day if you like: There's a cafe, sports bar, and pool room upstairs, and of course, endless video and arcade games. But if you're over 30, I'd bring earplugs. ⏱ *15 min. 1511 7th Ave.* ☎ *206/521-0952. www.gameworks.com. Mon–Thurs 11am–midnight; Fri 11am–1am; Sat 10am–1am; Sun 10am–midnight.*

❸ ★ **Pacific Place.** You can gaze at all four floors of this upscale, contemporary mall as you wind your way up the escalator to the 11-screen theater. The shops along the way are a who's who of retail: Barneys of New York, Eddie Bauer, Barnes & Noble, Cartier, J.Crew, Tiffany & Co., and Restoration Hardware. If you find yourself at Pacific Place at lunch or dinner time, you'll find several restaurants to choose from, including **Il Fornaio,** which serves fresh Italian fare in three locations, depending on your budget and time constraints: an atrium kiosk, a cafe, and a full-service restaurant. No matter where I'm going downtown, I always park at Pacific Place. It's centrally located, owned by the city, and one of the best deals in a town where parking is at a premium. At night, there's a special 4-hour rate of $4. ⏱ *1 hr. 6th Ave. & Pine St.* ☎ *206/405-2655. Most shops open Mon–Sat 10am–8pm; Sun 11am–6pm.*

❹ ★★ **Nordstrom.** The Nordstroms, one of Seattle's oldest families, moved their flagship store in 1998 from its cramped quarters to an empty 1918 building that was the former home of the iconic Frederick & Nelson department store. Nordstrom has come a long way since

Shop Savvy

It's easy to spend an entire morning or afternoon (or both) wandering through Pacific Place. But if you'd rather skip the national chain stores and hit the highlights, don't miss **O & Co.,** where you can sample exotic olive oils and other gourmet treats. Also be sure to stop in at the chic **Sixth Avenue Wine Seller,** where owner Beverly Shimada pours wines from around the world for $5 a glass during happy hour, from 4 to 6pm weekdays. And **Twist,** a Northwest boutique, is just plain fun. The colorful glassware and home decor items will lure you in; the unusual jewelry by artists around the world will keep you there longer than you'd planned.

Dotcom Delirium

Seattle has always been a boom-or-bust town, starting with the Gold Rush, and continuing much later with a series of massive hirings and devastating layoffs by Boeing. Then in the 1990s, strange things began happening in the once aviation-dependent economy. First, grunge rock grabbed the limelight for Seattle. Then a company named Microsoft, started by hometown boys Bill Gates and Paul Allen, mushroomed into a billion-dollar-a-year-plus business by 1990, helping to spawn an entire industry of dotcom startups. By the late '90s, Seattle's economy was flying high from the glorious infusion of dotcom dollars. World-class restaurants, theater, and other cultural activities sprang up or expanded, eager to fill the after-hour entertainment needs of the newly moneyed. Though the dotcom bubble burst in Seattle, and throughout the country, just a couple of years later, Seattle's now-diversified economy quickly revived and it remains one of the strongest in the nation.

Swedish immigrant John Nordstrom opened his first shoe store in 1901, using Gold Rush money he brought back from Alaska. My favorite story about the chain's legendary customer service is about a businessman who called the store from the airport years ago, in a panic because he didn't have a tie for a business meeting. A salesperson was dispatched to the airport with a selection of ties—or so the story goes. Considering Seattle's tangled traffic, I wouldn't count on the ties arriving in time these days, but the store's service is hard to beat. And, though today's Nordstrom is a full-service department store, the shoes are still exquisite. But before I try on a pair, I usually walk 3 blocks west to check out Nordstrom Rack (1601 2nd Ave.), where you can save up to 75% on clothing and shoes.
🕐 30 min. 500 Pine St. ☎ 206/628-2111. Mon–Sat 9:30am–9pm; Sun 11am–7pm.

⑤ ★★ **Westlake Center.** This is a chic mall, but with a comfy Seattle feel. I especially love browsing in the Seattle-based shops, such as Millstream, a Northwest arts and crafts boutique that looks like a mountain cabin; Romy, a home-grown, hip apparel shop; Fireworks, crammed with playful art; and Made in Washington, which sells souvenirs your friends will actually like. Seattle's mile-long monorail, built for the 1962 World's Fair, runs between Seattle Center and the top floor of Westlake Center. If your kids can't

Head to the escalators to check out the bronze plates on display in Macy's (p 64).

The shockingly chartreuse escalators at the Seattle Central Public Library.

take any more shopping, treat them to a quick ride for a break. ⏱ *1 hr. 400 Pine St. Mon–Thurs 10am–8pm; Fri–Sat 10am–9pm; Sun 11am–6pm.*

6 ★ kids **Food Court at West-lake.** This is a food court like none other I've seen. There's something to please every palate, from quesadillas to sushi, all amazingly fresh and tasty. It's easy on the family budget, and wiggleworms have plenty of room to stretch when they're done eating. A few highlights: Yeung's Lotus Express, Teriyaki Temple, Boba-chine Bubble Tea & Baguettes, Salena Mexicana, World Wraps, McKinley's Soup Plus, Sushi Bar, Mediterranean Avenue, and Emerald City Smoothie. *400 Pine Street, $.*

7 ★ **Macy's.** The famous high-end department store is ironically housed in the former Bon Marché, which for over 100 years catered to Seattle's working class. But look closely and you'll find traces of the old Bon. Check beside the escala-tors for the intricate 1929 bronze panels depicting industries of the

Northwest, from fisheries to technol-ogy. Look also for good clothing buys on the sales racks. ⏱ *15 min. 1601 3rd Ave.* ☎ *206/506-6000. Mon–Sat 10am–8pm; Sun 11am–7pm.*

8 ★ **Monorail Espresso.** My favorite downtown spot for a caf-feine break is Monorail Espresso, where you can drink in a little his-tory with your double latte. *520 Pike St. (at 5th).* ☎ *206/625-0449. $. See p 40.*

9 **City Centre.** This mixed-use building is a prestigious downtown office address, but it also houses some great little shops and, on the top retail floor, an excellent restau-rant (Palomino—with both a cafe and fine-dining room). But the best thing about City Centre is its daz-zling glass collection by the famed Pilchuck Glass School. Don't miss the life-size glass dinosaur skeleton. You'll also find a small food court on the lower floor. At Soups! I can never decide between the yummy chicken noodle and the portobello and roasted tomato bisque. Usually I ask for a sample of one, and buy a bowl of the other. At Juice Plant, you can get smoothies and sandwiches. ⏱ *15 min. 1420 5th Ave. Mon–Thurs, Sat 10am–6pm; Fri 10am–7pm; Sun 11am–5pm.*

⑩ ★★ **Benaroya Hall.** Home to the Seattle Symphony, Benaroya is a modernist dream. I highly recommend catching a concert here, but even if you're not in the mood for classical music, the hall is worth a peek. Check out the wonderfully fluid glass chandeliers by world-famous Seattle glass artist Dale Chihuly. ⏱ *30 min. 200 University St.* ☎ *206/215-4800. www.seattlesymphony.org. Ticket prices vary; free admission to see the chandeliers. See p 26.*

⑪ ★★★ **Seattle Art Museum.** Seattleites take their art seriously, and the SAM is a reflection of that. The museum is home to an outstanding array of works from all over the world, but be sure to check out the Northwest Native American collection, which is one of the finest you'll find anywhere. ⏱ *90 min. 1300 1st Ave.* ☎ *206/654-3100. www.seattleartmuseum.org. Admission $13 adults, $10 seniors over 62, $7 students & kids 13–17, free for kids 12 & under. Tues–Sun*

The Seattle Art Museum has an outstanding collection of Native American art.

10am–5pm; Thurs–Fri 10am–9pm. See p 26.

⑫ ★★★ kids **Seattle Central Public Library.** It's hard to say which is more fun: admiring the building or browsing its well-stocked shelves. One thing is for sure: You'll have to drag the kids out of the children's section. And yes, you can get a latte here. *1000 4th Ave.* ☎ *206/386-4636. www.spl.org. Free admission. Mon–Thurs 10am–8pm; Fri–Sat 10am–6pm; Sun noon–6pm. See p 46.*

Cai Guo-Qiang's massive work greets visitors to the Seattle Art Museum.

Capitol Hill

1 Volunteer Park
2 Harvard-Belmont Landmark District
3 Consignment Apparel Shops
4 Dance Footsteps
5 Espresso Vivace
6 Seattle Museum of the Mysteries
7 Noah's New York Bagels
8 Museum of History & Industry

Remnants of the grunge era live on in this eclectic neighborhood, which is also the center of gay life in Seattle. In addition to jet-black attire and gratuitous piercings, expect to see the occasional neon-blue Mohawk, cross-dressing shoppers, and panhandlers who may at times be a bit unsteady on their feet. The housing is also diverse, with seedy apartments sharing space with spectacular mansions. Likewise, the shops along Broadway range from retro consignment to ultratrendy fashion. It's safe to bring young children here, but except for Volunteer Park—far removed from the Broadway street scene—there's not much of interest for them. START: **Bus 10 or 12 to Volunteer Park.**

1 ★★ kids Volunteer Park.

Flush with Gold Rush money, Seattle hired the famous Olmsted Brothers (John Charles Olmsted was the stepson of Frederick Law Olmsted, who designed New York City's Central Park) in 1903 to design an elaborate series of parks, one of the best in the country. One of these is Volunteer Park. There's lots of room to run and trails to explore at this urban oasis. If you climb the 106 indoor steps to the top of the Water Tower at the south end of the park, you'll be rewarded with one of the best views in town. But if you're out of breath by the time you climb the two flights to the entrance, don't even bother! Just west of the tower is the Seattle Asian Art Museum (p 28). Walk farther west and you'll see the beautiful Volunteer Park Conservatory, bursting with color from exotic

An exotic bloom at Volunteer Park Conservatory.

tropical plants, including a large orchid collection. You'd hardly be surprised if a parrot landed on your shoulder. ⏲ *1 hr. 1400 E. Galer St. Volunteer Park Conservatory ☎ 206/ 684-4743. www.seattle.gov/parks. Free admission. Daily 10am–4pm; Memorial Day–Labor Day 10am–7pm.*

The greenhouse at Volunteer Park.

② Harvard-Belmont Landmark District. Seattle has more than its share of millionaires—both dotcom and otherwise—and quite a few of them live in this tree-shaded historic neighborhood. The area is filled with graceful, sprawling mansions built in the early part of the twentieth century. The best walk is along the northern end of Broadway, between East Highland and East Roy. You can also drive along these roads, but walking allows for better peeking through the hedges. ⏱ *30 min. Bounded roughly by Harvard Ave., Broadway, Bellevue Place & Boylston.*

③ Consignment Apparel Shops. With two colleges nearby (Seattle University and Seattle Central Community College), previously worn—and retro—clothing is highly sought after. There aren't as many vintage apparel shops as there once were along Broadway, but the ones that remain are excellent. **Crossroads Trading Co.** (325 Broadway E; ☎ 206/328-5867) focuses on contemporary styles. Some items are new, but the only way to tell is by their blue tags. This is not the cheapest consignment shop in town, but the merchandise is top-flight. **Metro Clothing Company** (231 Broadway

Pick up some funky footwear at Metro Clothing in Capitol Hill.

Take a moment to add a little dance to your day.

E; ☎ 206/726-7978) is also an excellent spot for fashion finds. ⏱ *1 hr. Broadway E.*

④ Dance Footsteps. One of the most unusual displays of public art you'll find in Seattle is embedded in the sidewalks along Broadway. Dancers' Series: Steps consists of bronze shoeprints—the soles of the shoes, that is—of dancers performing various dance steps. There are eight sets along the avenue, from the tango to the foxtrot, and a couple of steps that artist Jack Mackie made up just for fun. Try them out! No need to feel self-conscious—it takes a lot to turn heads on Capitol Hill. ⏱ *15 min. Along Broadway.*

⑤ ★★ Espresso Vivace. This is a no-frills stand, but the coffee drinks are sublime, right down to the rosetta pattern the barista "draws" in the foam. Sidewalk seating is available, and it's a perfect spot for people-watching. My favorite: the rich, creamy caffe caramel. *321 Broadway Ave. E. (See p 41, ⑧.)*

⑥ Seattle Museum of the Mysteries. Northwesterners spend a great deal of time pondering the reality (or lack thereof) of Bigfoot. No need to look further than here. Peer down at the below-sidewalk entrance to this quirky museum and you'll see the legendary creature seated outside—at

Who doesn't love Bigfoot? Stop in and say hi at the Museum of Mysteries.

least an overgrown stuffed version. Inside, things get stranger still. The collection includes books, photos, and recordings of all things paranormal—including reports of various hauntings around Seattle, like the much-rumored Pike Place Market ghost. There's also an oxygen bar, purported to combat allergies and hangovers. After closing from 10pm to midnight every Saturday, and every second, third, and fourth Friday of the month, play Ghost Poker with antique chips at the Mystery Museum Lock In ($5 suggested donation adults, $3 ages 8–16, free for those 7 and under).
🕐 30 min. ☎ 206/328-6499. www. seattlechatclub.org. 623 Broadway Ave. E. Admission $2 suggested donation adults, $1 ages 9–17, free for those under 9. Mon–Thurs noon–8:30pm; Fri–Sat noon–10pm.

7 Noah's New York Bagels. It may not be a West Coast thing, but if you have a hankering for a bagel, you'll find a good variety here. I like the asiago. And since Noah's knows how to do coffee Seattle-style, you can down it with a creamy caramel macchiato. *220 Broadway E. ☎ 206/ 720-2925. $.*

8 ★★ Museum of History & Industry (MOHAI). This museum, which opened in 1952, is operated by the Seattle Historical Association and its fascinating collection will give you an excellent overview of the Northwest's history. The core exhibit focuses on Seattle and tells the city's story through pictures, artifacts, and oral histories. 🕐 1 hr. 2700 24th Ave E. ☎ 206/324-1126. www.seattlehistory.org. Admission $7 adults, $5 ages 5–17 & seniors, free 4 & under. Also free 1st Thurs of the month. Daily 10am–5pm, 1st Thurs of the month 10am–8pm. See p 24.

Bigfoot

The most popular legend in the Northwest, without a doubt, is that of Sasquatch, more fondly dubbed Bigfoot. Does the creature exist or doesn't he? Depends who you ask. Believers swear that Sasquatches roam the forests and mountains of the Pacific Northwest; doubters scoff. Reports of an enormous hairy beast in the region have been circulating since the early 1800s. Some, but not all, of the stories have been proven to be fraudulent. In 1969, a man in northern Washington reported finding Sasquatch footprints in a ghost town called Bossburg. Bigfoot hunters rushed to the scene and found additional tracks nearby—more than 1,000 in all. One of them was measured at more than 17 inches long. At least one British anthropologist was impressed with the find. Sasquatch-spotters often report an awful, skunklike smell just before they see the beast or its tracks. But with no scientifically confirmed hard proof, the mystery—and perhaps the ape-man—lives on.

Chinatown/Int'l District

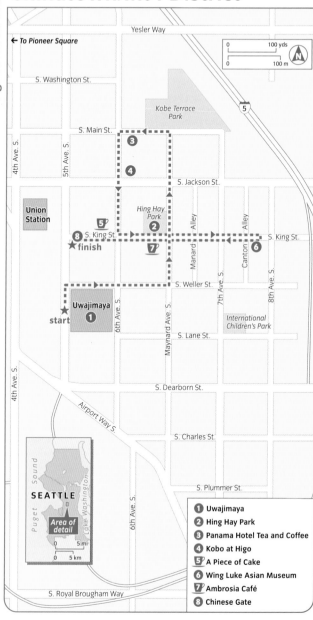

Yesler Way

← To Pioneer Square

0   100 yds
0   100 m

S. Washington St.

Kobe Terrace Park

5

S. Main St.

4th Ave. S.
5th Ave. S.

3

4

S. Jackson St.

Union Station

5 A Piece of Cake

Hing Hay Park

2

Alley

Manard

Alley

Canton

8 ★ finish

S. King St.

7

S. King St.

6

S. Weller St.

6th Ave. S.

Maynard Ave. S.

7th Ave. S.

8th Ave. S.

★ start

Uwajimaya

1

International Children's Park

S. Lane St.

S. Dearborn St.

4th Ave. S.

Airport Way S.

S. Charles St.

SEATTLE

Puget Sound

Lake Washington

Area of detail

0   5 mi
0   5 km

S. Plummer St.

6th Ave. S.

S. Royal Brougham Way

1 Uwajimaya
2 Hing Hay Park
3 Panama Hotel Tea and Coffee
4 Kobo at Higo
5 A Piece of Cake
6 Wing Luke Asian Museum
7 Ambrosia Café
8 Chinese Gate

Though not as large as San Francisco's Chinatown, this Asian neighborhood is lively—and about as diverse as they come, with a flood of Southeast Asian immigrants joining the mix in recent years. Its name has morphed (after sometimes bitter disputes) from Chinatown to International District to the current compromise: Chinatown/International District. When I feel like globetrotting but can't spare the time, I'll spend an afternoon here, strolling past rows of whole barbecued ducks hanging by their feet, riotously colorful vegetable markets spilling out into the streets, window displays of exotic herbs and medicines, and pastry shops hawking some of the tastiest goods in town. It's all about the smells, the colors, and the single-minded shoppers tracking down bargains. START: **Bus 26, 28, 39, or 42.**

❶ ★★ Uwajimaya. Yes, it's a grocery store, but this is also a bona fide tourist destination. Built by a Japanese patriarch whose family was interned during World War II, this enormous supermarket—now run by his children—is stocked with exotic Asian produce, meats, baked goods, and other products. You can sign up for a cooking class (learn to make sushi!) or just browse. There is also an Asian bookstore, gift shop, and a large dine-in area that gives an entirely new meaning to the term "food court." ⏱ *1 hr.* ☎ *206/624-6248. 600 5th Ave. S. Mon–Sat 9am–10pm; Sun 9am–9pm.*

❷ Hing Hay Park. This small but unusual park is situated on a red-bricked square. The colorful pagoda, crafted in Taipei, Taiwan, is the genuine article, as is the spectacular dragon artwork. If you have time, settle in at one of the chess tables for a leisurely game. The city is in the process of doubling the size of the park, a popular gathering spot that often hosts the Lunar New Year Lion Dances in February. ⏱ *15 min. 423 Maynard Ave. S. (King St. & Maynard).*

❸ ★ Panama Hotel Tea and Coffee. You can sip Italian LAvAzzA coffee or choose from a global tea menu at this elegant shop in the

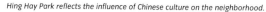

Hing Hay Park reflects the influence of Chinese culture on the neighborhood.

The Best Neighborhood Walks

Trunks left behind by Japanese families sent to internment camps during WWII are a reminder of a painful past.

historic Panama Hotel, which was home to Japanese workingmen in the early 20th century. The hotel basement was once a Japanese bathhouse, and tours are available (see box below). When current owner Jan Johnson bought the hotel, she discovered trunks full of personal items left behind and never reclaimed by Japanese families sent off to internment camps during World War II. You can view one of these trunks through a glass window in the tea shop's wooden floor. Many other items are on display as a history lesson and a reminder of a regrettable moment in time. ⏱ 30 min. 607 S. Main St. ☎ 206/515-4000. www.panamahotel seattle.com.

❹ ★ **Kobo at Higo.** History stands still at this shop, housed in the former Higo Variety Store, a Japanese five-and-dime that stood in this spot for 75 years. The Murakami family had to board it up while they were sent to an internment camp, but

reopened when they returned. Sadly, the father died very shortly afterward, but his widow and children kept it going until 2003, when the youngest daughter retired. Happily, the new owners, John Bisbee and Binko Chiong-Bisbee, have preserved much of the past, including pre-war merchandise and family mementos. Be sure to check out the display wall devoted to the old Higo. The Bisbees have also brought stylish new treasures to the shop, which they have turned into a Japanese and Northwest art and craft gallery. ⏱ 30 min. ☎ 206/381-3000. www.koboseattle. com. 604 S. Jackson St. Mon–Sat 11am–6pm.

❺ ★★ **A Piece of Cake.** This is my favorite bakery in Seattle. The cakes are feather-light, the frosting flavorful but not too sweet, and the fillings creative. My favorite, in season, is the melon-ball-filled cake. Yum! The cakes here are works of art, perfect for a very special occasion. Other times, I usually order a cup of tea and a pineapple bun. ⏱ 30 min. ☎ 206/623-8284. 514 S. King St. Daily 9am–9pm. $.

❻ ★★ **Wing Luke Asian Museum.** This Smithsonian Institution–affiliated museum, one of the best of its kind in the nation, is a great community resource in the midst of a surprisingly diverse neighborhood. Its library, which is open to

Happily, the desserts at A Piece of Cake taste as good as they look.

Kobo at Higo is more than a shop—it offers a glimpse into the area's past.

District to specialize in pearl tea, a craze that started in Taiwan. Now available all over town—and more often called "bubble tea"—the icy drink consists of brewed tea mixed with sweetened milk and syrups, poured into a tall cup filled with gumball-size tapioca balls. You drink it through a straw wide enough to suck up the "bubbles." It's an odd sensation the first time or two, but then you get hooked. Try the mango and green tea flavors. ☎ 206/623-9028. 619 S. King St. 11am–8pm. $.

the public during museum hours, includes a wealth of oral and video histories, photos, and books about the experiences of Asian Pacific Americans in the Northwest. *719 S. King St. (S. King St. & 8th Ave. S.).* ☎ 206/623-5124. www.wingluke. org. $4 adults, $3 seniors & students, $2 ages 5–12. Tues–Fri 11am–4:30pm; Sat–Sun noon–4pm. See p 24.

7 Ambrosia Café. This was the first shop in the International

8 Chinese Gate. After a half-century of grass-roots efforts, Seattle's Chinatown finally has its own traditional entrance gate, just like other major cities with large Chinese populations, such as San Francisco and Los Angeles. The eye-catching, 45-foot (14m) archway was just unveiled in 2008. According to tradition, the $500,000 gate should bring luck and strength. It also greets visitors and makes it easier to spot the district. There are hopes of building a second gate on the other end of the neighborhood. *S. King St., just east of 5th Ave. S.*

Bathhouse Tour

When early Japanese immigrants came to the United States, they built hundreds of community bathhouses, just like those they used at home. The bathhouses, or sentos, were culturally important places to socialize, relax in the hot water, and clean off after a hard day's work. Only one remains intact in its original location, and that is the marble bath in the basement of the Panama Hotel in Seattle. It officially closed in 1950, but is still open for historic tours. To schedule one, call Jan Johnson at ☎ 206/223-9242.

Limerick County Library

Fremont

SEATTLE

Area of detail

Phinney Ave. N.

Puget Sound

Lake Washington

Evanston Ave. N.

Fremont Ave. N.

Fremont Pl.

N. 36th St.   start

FREMONT

N. 35th St.

Aurora Ave. N.

finish

N. 34th St.

N. Northlake Way

Lake Washington Ship Canal

Fremont Ave. N.

QUEEN ANNE

Fremont Bridge

George Washington Bridge

Lake Union

99

① (under bridge)

① Fremont Troll
② Statue of Lenin
③ Fremont Rocket
④ Peet's Coffee & Tea
⑤ PCC Natural Markets
⑥ *Waiting for the Interurban* Statue

The self-proclaimed center of the universe (with a sign to prove it), this funky north-end neighborhood has a quirkiness that several years of gentrification have failed to destroy. Tech firms Adobe Systems and Getty have built their headquarters here, and high-end condos followed. Though some of the cottage-industry art studios have given way to higher-rent tenants, this is still an artsy kind of place. One of my favorite things about Fremont is the eccentric public art scattered about the neighborhood. When I'm not in the mood for the urban pace of shopping downtown, I head for friendly, relaxed Fremont. START: **Under the north end of the Aurora Avenue Bridge, at N. 36th St.**

① ★★ kids **Fremont Troll.** If you drive over the Aurora Avenue Bridge, hope your car doesn't suffer the same fate as the Volkswagen Bug plucked off the road by the nasty-tempered troll lurking below. At least, that's how the story goes. The 18-foot-high (5.5m) troll, which

reflects the neighborhood's Scandinavian roots, is much friendlier if you visit him in person. You can climb on him all you want, and he's okay with family pictures, too. Back in 1989, when the Fremont Arts Council held a nationwide search for a piece of public art to go under the

Yes, that rocket was once property of the U.S. Army.

bridge, Fremont residents overwhelmingly voted for the troll. ⏱ *15 min. N. 36th St., under the Aurora Avenue Bridge, also known as the George Washington Memorial Bridge.*

❷ ★ **Statue of Lenin.** We're talking Vladimir. The sculpture of the

Stop by and say hi to Vl Lenin.

former Russian revolutionary ended up in Fremont on a fluke, and here it has stayed, despite controversy. It was brought back from Slovakia by a Seattle-area bronze artist who was considering selling it for scrap when he met with an untimely death. His family had the statue moved near a brass foundry in Fremont, and no one has figured out what to do with it since. Now it's become a part of this eccentric neighborhood where hardly anything seems out of place. If you're here during a holiday season, expect to see Lenin decked out in appropriate garb. ⏱ *15 min. 36th St. & Evanston Ave. N.*

❸ ★ **Fremont Rocket.** It's an odd twist of fate that the statue of Lenin ended up just down the block from a 55-foot (17m) for-real Cold War–era rocket, taken from an Army surplus store, mounted on a building in Fremont, and—voilà!—turned into art. Stop by in the evening to see the rocket's onboard lights ablaze. ⏱ *15 min. 36th St. & Evanston Ave. N.*

Commuters everywhere can relate to Waiting for the Interurban.

4 **Peet's Coffee & Tea.** There's often a line at this popular coffee shop, but it usually moves fast and it's worth the wait. I go there when I'm craving a hazelnut latte. If you've had enough coffee for the day, Peet's also has a good selection of teas, and a nice assortment of pastries for your sweet tooth. There are several branches of this chain in Seattle. *3401 Fremont Ave. N. $.*

5 **PCC Natural Markets.** Fruits and veggies have never been so much fun, and these are bursting with flavor, much of it from local farms. PCC is an all-organic store with a produce section so irresistible, I'll go out of my way to shop here. Kids get free fruit, so be sure to ask. This is a full-service grocery store, and all the cosmetic and fragrance products are animal-cruelty-free. It's technically a co-op, but nonmembers can shop here, too. I can never pass by the bakery, which features such unusual items as Paris balsamic pear tarts—a personal favorite—and vegan carrot cake, without making a pit stop. *600 N. 34th St.* ☎ *206/632-6811.*

6 ★ *Waiting for the Interurban.* Six passengers and a dog wait endlessly for their train in this cast-aluminum sculpture memorializing the era of the electric rail line. It also memorializes a squabble between the sculptor, local resident Richard Beyer, and Fremont political leader Armen Stepanian: If you look closely, you'll see that the dog has a human face. That would be Stepanian's. And unless you look closely, you might mistake the riders for real people, as pranksters are fond of dressing the statues, often in seasonal attire. ⏱ *15 min. South side of N. 34th St.* ●

Shopping **Best Bets**

Best **Art Jewelry**
★★★ Twist, *600 Pine St. (p 89)*

Best **Bookstore (New)**
★★★ Elliott Bay Book Company, *101 S. Main St. (p 84)*

Best **Bookstore (Used)**
★★ Twice Sold Tales, *905 E. John St. (p 84)*

Best **Gifts**
★★★ FireWorks, *210 1st Ave. S. (p 88)*

Best **Glass**
★★★ Glasshouse Studio, *311 Occidental Ave. S. (p 90)*

Best **Hand-crafted Wood Furniture**
★★ Northwest Fine Woodworking, *101 S. Jackson St. (p 87)*

Best **Pirates' Booty**
Pirates Plunder, *1301 Alaskan Way (p 89)*

Best **Place to Buy a Musical Instrument**
★★ Lark in the Morning Musique Shoppe, *1401 1st Ave. (p 91)*

Best **Rugs**
★ Palace Rug Gallery, *323 1st Ave. S. (p 92)*

Best **Fashion Bargains**
★★★ Nordstrom Rack, *1601 2nd Ave. (p 85)*

Best **Place to Find a Manly Skirt**
★ Utilikilts, *620 1st Ave. (p 87)*

Best **Spot to Find an Obscure Magazine**
★★ Broadway News, *204 Broadway Ave. (p 84)*

Best **Shoes**
★★★ Nordstrom, *500 Pine St. (p 85)*

Best **Souvenirs**
★★ Made in Washington, *400 Pine St. (p 88)*

Best **Place to Buy a Gown for the Opera**
★★ Mario's, *513 6th Ave. (p 86)*

Best **Toys**
★★ Magic Mouse Toys, *603 1st Ave. (p 92)*

Glass as works of art at Glasshouse Studios.

Downtown Shopping

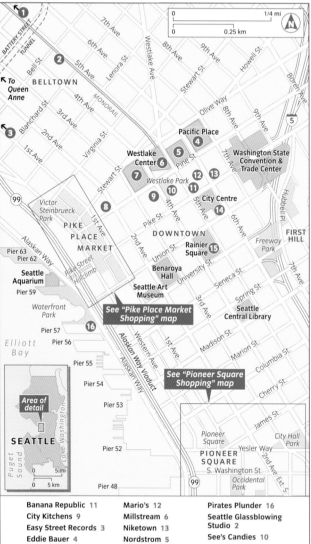

Banana Republic 11	Mario's 12	Pirates Plunder 16
City Kitchens 9	Millstream 6	Seattle Glassblowing
Easy Street Records 3	Niketown 13	Studio 2
Eddie Bauer 4	Nordstrom 5	See's Candies 10
Jeffrey Moose	Nordstrom Rack 8	Silver Platters 1
Gallery 15	Pacific Place 4	Twist 4
Lush Cosmetics 6	Pelindaba Lavender	Westlake Center 6
Macy's 7	Gallery 14	

Pioneer Square Shopping

A.J. Smith & Co. Antiques 13
Agate Designs 7
Akanyi African & Tribal Art Gallery 24
The Clog Factory 15
The Cutty Sark 17
D'Adamo/Woltz Gallery 19
Elements Interiors 25
Elliott Bay Book Company 18
FireWorks 9
Flanagan & Lane Antiques 23
Foster/White 26
Glasshouse Studio 20
Globe Books 11

Golden Loom Rug Gallery 14
Lanna Trading Co. 6
Magic Mouse Toys 5
Megan Mary Olander Flowers 12
Noble Horse Gallery 10
Northwest Fine Woodworking 21
Palace Rug Gallery 16
Pioneer Square Antique Mall 3
Ragazzi's Flying Shuttle 4
Seattle Mystery Bookshop 1
Seattle Soapworks 22
Synapse 206 8
Utilikilts 2

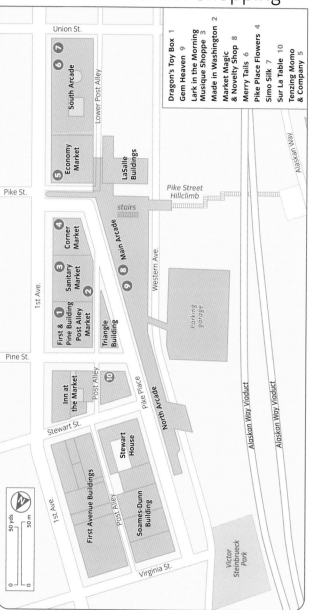

Pike Place Market Shopping

Dragon's Toy Box 1
Gem Heaven 9
Lark in the Morning
Musique Shoppe 3
Made in Washington 2
Market Magic
& Novelty Shop 8
Merry Tails 6
Pike Place Flowers 4
Simo Silk 7
Sur La Table 10
Tenzing Momo
& Company 5

Union St.

Lower Post Alley

South Arcade

⑥ ⑦

Economy Market

⑤

LaSalle Buildings

Pike St.

Alaskan Way

Pike Street Hillclimb

stairs

Corner Market ④

Sanitary Market ③

First & Pine Building Post Alley Market ① ②

Main Arcade ⑧

⑨

Western Ave.

Parking garage

1st Ave.

Triangle Building

Pine St.

Inn at the Market

Post Alley ⑩

Post Alley

Pike Place

North Arcade

Stewart St.

Stewart House

Alaskan Way Viaduct

Alaskan Way Viaduct

First Avenue Buildings

Soames-Dunn Building

Post Alley

1st Ave.

Virginia St.

Victor Steinbrueck Park

N

50 yds
50 m

0
0

Capitol Hill Shopping

Area of detail

SEATTLE

Puget Sound

Lake Washington

0   5 mi
0   5 km

Bailey/Coy Books 5
Blooms on Broadway 6
Broadway News 3
Crossroads Trading Co. 8
Dilettante Mocha Café 4
Kobo 2
The Metro Clothing Co. 10

Mud Bay Granary 9
Panache 11
Presence: Art of Living 1
Trendy Wendy 12
Twice Sold Tales 13
Urban Outfitters 7
Wall of Sound 14

Shopping **A to Z**

Antiques

★ A.J. Smith & Co. Antiques

PIONEER SQUARE My favorite thing to do at this shop in the Grand Central Arcade is leaf through the vintage magazines, postcards, and antique photos. The glass and china are also worth a look. *89 S. Washington St.* ☎ *206/624-9104. Bus: 15, 18, 21, 22, 56. Map p 80.*

The Cutty Sark PIONEER SQUARE

Nautical antiques—from compasses to ship's wheels—are sold here, making it the perfect place to grab gifts for all the old salts on your list. *320 1st Ave. S.* ☎ *206/262-1265. ww.cuttyantiques.com. AE, DISC, MC, V. Bus: 15, 18, 21, 22, 56. Map p 80.*

★ Flanagan & Lane Antiques PIONEER

SQUARE The French furniture is exquisite; so are the colorful Chinese fans and

Flanagan & Lane Antiques features fine china and glassware, among other items.

dishes. Don't miss the interesting assortment of antique clocks. The focus is on the 17th through 20th centuries. *165 S. Jackson St.* ☎ *206/ 682-0098. AE, DISC, MC, V. Bus: 99. Map p 80.*

★ Pioneer Square Antique Mall

PIONEER SQUARE Looking for a Shirley Temple doll? A princess phone? You're likely to find them here in the basement of the historic Pioneer Building. Be sure to give yourself time to explore the labyrinth of rooms burrowed beneath the modern-day sidewalks. *602 1st Ave.* ☎ *206/624-1164. www.pioneerbuilding.com/antique_mall.htm. DISC, MC, V. Bus: 16, 99. Map p 80.*

Art

★★ Akanyi African & Tribal Art Gallery

PIONEER SQUARE African and tribal art are showcased at this unique shop, which features a large collection of musical instruments, masks, and furniture from the various regions of Africa. *155 S. Main St.* ☎ *206/381-3133. www.akanyiafricanart.com. AE, MC, V. Bus 99. Map p 80.*

★★ D'Adamo/Woltz Gallery

PIONEER SQUARE In this light and airy studio, contemporary art is the focus, with an emphasis on sculpture and painting. The featured artists are generally well known worldwide, but during the gallery's annual February exhibition the spotlight is on local emerging talent. *307 Occidental Ave S.* ☎ *206/652-4414. www.dadamowoltzgallery.com. AE, MC, V. Bus 99. Map p 80.*

Stop by the D'Adamo/Woltz Gallery for a glimpse of their modern art.

★★ Jeffrey Moose Gallery

DOWNTOWN This eclectic shop specializes in indigenous art, including Australian aboriginal works and Native American masks and carvings. It also has a great selection of glass, paintings, and prints by artists from the Northwest and around the world. *1333 5th Ave., Ste. 511.* ☎ *206/467-6951. www. jeffreymoosegallery.com. AE, MC, V. Bus: 2. Map p 79.*

Books & Magazines
★ Bailey/Coy Books CAPITOL

HILL This terrific little neighborhood bookstore doesn't shy away from controversial titles. Readers whose politics tilt toward the left will especially enjoy Bailey/Coy. *414 Broadway Ave. E.* ☎ *206/323-8842. www.baileycoybooks.com. AE, DISC, MC, V. Bus: 49. Map p 82.*

★★ Broadway News CAPITOL

HILL One of the best selections of magazines to be found; it's hard to imagine a title they don't stock, from music to politics. You will also find newspapers from around the world. *204 Broadway Ave.* ☎ *206/324-7323. AE, MC, V. Bus: 49. Map p 82.*

★★★ kids Elliott Bay Book

Company PIONEER SQUARE Seattle's premier bookstore is a must-do for any bibliophile. You could easily spend the better part of an afternoon exploring and still feel like you might have missed something. See p 15. *101 S. Main St.* ☎ *206/624-6600. www.elliottbaybook.com. AE, DISC, MC, V. Bus: 15, 18, 21, 22, 56. Map p 80.*

★ Globe Books PIONEER SQUARE

From Beowulf to Harry Potter, you're likely to find what you're looking for in this wonderfully musty shop. They tracked down a cookbook I'd been hunting for for years—and charged me less than half the price I'd seen on e-Bay. *218 1st Ave. S.* ☎ *206/*

Mystery buffs will want to set aside plenty of time for the Seattle Mystery Bookshop.

682-6882. DISC, MC, V. Bus: 15, 18, 21, 22, 56. Map p 80.

★ Seattle Mystery Bookshop

PIONEER SQUARE Skullduggery reigns supreme here. Word of warning to mystery-lovers: This will-not be a quick stop for you. And good luck stumping the well-informed staff. *117 Cherry St.* ☎ *206/587-5737. www.seattlemystery.com. MC, V. Bus: 15, 18, 21, 22, 56. Map p 80.*

★★ Twice Sold Tales CAPITOL

HILL You'd be hard-pressed to find a deeper inventory of used books. Plan to browse. And if you're a cat-lover, figure in some time to play with the kitties that roam the shop as well. *Locations include: 905 E. John St.* ☎ *206/324-2421; 4501 University Way NE.* ☎ *206/545-4226. MC, V. Bus: 49. Map p 82.*

Candy
★★ Dilettante Mocha Café

CAPITOL HILL Sure, you could stop here for a dynamite mocha, but don't pass up the hand-dipped truffles and other candies, made with recipes passed down from the owners' great uncle, who prepared them for the Imperial Court of Austria. If your taste buds fall in love, you can join the shop's chocolate club and get treats delivered to your door every month. *Locations include: 416 Broadway E. ☎ 206/ 329-6463. www.dilettante.com. AE, DISC, MC, V. Bus: 49. Map p 82.*

★★ See's Candies DOWNTOWN See's offers scrumptious gourmet candies at a good value. The company has been around for 90 years or so, and it has come up with a variety of new tastes in addition to its tried-and-true favorites. For an unusual treat, bring home a box of their gourmet lollypops. *Downtown location: 1518 4th Ave. ☎ 206/682-7122. www.sees.com. AE, MC, V. Bus: 10. Map p 79.*

Department Stores
★★ Macy's DOWNTOWN High-end clothing, jewelry, housewares, and cosmetics are beautifully displayed in a historic Seattle building. Be sure to check out the sales racks. *1601 3rd Ave. ☎ 206/506-6000. www.macys.com. AE, MC, V. Bus: 11, 12, 49. Map p 79.*

★★★ Nordstrom DOWNTOWN The shoes! Nordstrom got its start over a century ago as a humble Seattle shoe store and, while it's hardly humble anymore, it's still those fabulous shoes that lure me in. Of course, there's much, much more, including beautiful children's clothes. Everything is high quality, with high price tags to match. But watch for Nordstrom's legendary Half Yearly sales. *500 Pine St. ☎ 206/628-2111. www. nordstrom.com. AE, DISC, MC, V. Bus: 11, 12, 49. Map p 79.*

Discount/Consignment Shopping
Crossroads Trading Co. CAPITOL HILL Not all the clothes here are used, but the only way to tell is by the tags, because everything looks new and hip. This is not the cheapest consignment shop in town, but you'll find truly great stuff here. *325 Broadway E. ☎ 206/328-5867. www.crossroadstrading.com. MC, V. Bus: 49. Map p 82.*

★★★ Nordstrom Rack DOWNTOWN You'll have to do some hunting, but that's part of the fun. Amid the racks and racks of clothes, housewares, and, yes, shoes!—are usually a few treasures waiting to be

Stock up on fabulous fashions at Trendy Wendy (p 87).

Yes, it's a chain, but that doesn't mean you won't find unique and funky fashions at Urban Outfitters.

discovered. *1601 2nd Ave.* ☎ *206/448-8522. www.nordstrom.com. AE, DISC, MC, V. Bus: 15, 18, 21, 22, 56. Map p 79.*

Fashion

Banana Republic DOWNTOWN It's a great place to find khakis, denim, and other casual attire. *500 Pike St.* ☎ *206/622-2303. www.bananarepublic.com. AE, DISC, MC, V. Bus: 10. Map p 79.*

Eddie Bauer DOWNTOWN This Northwest-based company specializes, fittingly, in sportswear for men and women and outdoor gear. You can also find business casual attire and bedding. This one is on the second floor of Pacific Place. *600 Pine St., Ste. 230.* ☎ *206/622-2766. www.eddiebauer.com. AE, DISC, MC, V. Bus: 11, 12, 49. Map p 79.*

★★ Mario's DOWNTOWN For that perfect evening gown, if money is no object, you're sure to find a jaw-dropper here. The men's clothing is also exceptional. Everything is beautifully tailored, and the service equally impeccable. *513 6th Ave.*

☎ *206/622-6161. www.marios.com. AE, DISC, MC, V. Bus: 10. Map p 79.*

The Metro Clothing Co. CAPITOL HILL This shop is for the painfully hip only (except at Halloween!). If you're looking for leather and lace, Goth fashion, or thigh-high red boots with heels, this is the place to come. *231 Broadway E.* ☎ *206/726-7978. MC, V. Bus: 49. Map p 82.*

Panache CAPITOL HILL The name fits—the clothing here is trendy but elegant, and the jewelry and shoes make perfect accompaniments. There's a separate men's section. You can pick up some unusual gifts while you're here. *225 Broadway E.* ☎ *206/726-3300. MC, V. Bus: 49. Map p 82.*

Presence: Art of Living CAPITOL HILL Here, you'll find very hip clothes and shoes that actually fit comfortably on real people. There is also an eclectic mix of soaps, candles, and other gifts. *713 Broadway E.* ☎ *206/325-5330. MC, V. Bus: 49. Map p 82.*

★ Ragazzi's Flying Shuttle PIONEER SQUARE The art is wearable at this shop, which offers hand-woven apparel and accessories, and a fun collection of original

In the market for a shoe-shaped chair? Head to Elements Interiors.

contemporary jewelry. *607 1st Ave.*
☎ *206/343-9762. www.ragazzis
flyingshuttle.com. MC, V. Bus: 3, 4,
16, 99. Map p 80.*

★ **Simo Silk** PIKE PLACE MARKET
Named for the owner's sons, Simeon
and Moses, this shop offers a large
selection of buttery soft, mostly
washable silk shirts, scarves, and
jackets from Asia. The prices are
reasonable. The store has been so
successful, John Man has opened a
second one in Pioneer Square. *1411
1st Ave. #108.* ☎ *206/521-8816.
www.simosilk.com. MC, V. Bus: 15,
18, 21, 22, 56. Map p 81.*

★★ **Synapse 206** PIONEER
SQUARE   Tina Beuche's shop car-
ries some of the hippest clothing in
town. She sells local designers' creations, plus some ready-to-wear
items. The colors draw you into the
store; the styles keep you browsing.
206 1st Ave. S. ☎ *206/447-7731.
www.synapse206.com. AE, DISC,
MC, V. Bus: 15, 18, 21, 22, 56.
Map p 80.*

Trendy Wendy CAPITOL HILL
You'll get the red-carpet welcome
here, literally, at this boutique,
which features very hip clothes and
accessories. And there's even a
plus-size section. *211 Broadway E.*
☎ *206/322-6642. AE, DISC, MC, V.
Bus: 49. Map p 82.*

★ **Urban Outfitters** CAPITOL HILL
Whether you're looking for casual
chic attire or anything you'd need to
accessorize an urban loft, you're
likely to find it here. There's also an
assortment of irreverent gifts with a
left-wing bent. *401 Broadway E.
(in the Broadway Market).* ☎ *206/
322-1800. www.urbanoutfittersinc.
com. AE, DISC, MC, V. Bus: 49.
Map p 82.*

★ **Utilikilts** PIONEER SQUARE
If the slogan "Free Your Balls and
Free Yourself" appeals, you'll want
to check out these liberating kilts for

*Rock collectors rejoice! Even noncollec-
tors will enjoy checking out Agate
Designs (p 88) cool offerings.*

men. There are eight basic styles, all
handmade; custom orders cost
extra. Utilikilts were designed by a
Seattle man who now sells them in a
number of stores around the U.S.
and in Canada. *620 1st Ave.* ☎ *206/
282-4226. www.utilikilts.com. AE,
DISC, MC, V. Bus: 15, 18, 21, 22, 56.
Map p 80.*

Furniture
★ **Elements Interiors** PIONEER
SQUARE   You'll find ultrahip furnish-
ings here, such as chairs in fun
shapes. My favorite? The giant high
heel. Everything, even the leather
sofas, comes with a splash of creativity. These items are perfect for an
urban loft. *320 2nd Ave S.* ☎ *206/
622-3001. www.elementshome
interiors.com. AE, DISC, MC, V.
Bus: 99. Map p 80.*

★★ **Northwest Fine Wood-
working** PIONEER SQUARE   The
contemporary furniture and decor
items feature stunning blended
woods. The price tags are high, but
so is the quality. *101 S. Jackson St.*
☎ *206/625-0542. www.nwfinewood
working.com. AE, DISC, MC, V.
Bus: 99. Map p 80.*

Gems

★ kids **Agate Designs** PIONEER SQUARE   A 300-pound amethyst geode might be a bit large for your house, but a pair of bookends or a small fountain might be just right. The bowls, jewelry, and other items sold here are made from dazzling gems, minerals, and fossils. *120 1st Ave. S.* ☎ *206/621-3063. www.agate designs.com. AE, MC, V. Bus: 15, 18, 21, 22, 56. Map p 80.*

kids **Gem Heaven** PIKE PLACE MARKET   You'll find a large selection of minerals, gems, and jewelry in this shop "Down Under" at the Market. *1501 Pike Place #408.* ☎ *206/381-9302. AE, MC, V. Bus: 15, 18, 21, 22, 56. Map p 81.*

Gifts

★★★ kids **Fireworks** PIONEER SQUARE   This playful shop is my favorite gift destination. Whether it's for a wedding, baby shower, birthday, or holiday, I always find something just right. There are two themes at Fireworks: whimsy and inspiration, and often a combination of the two. Check out the revolving shadow lanterns, handmade by Northwest artists. *210 1st Ave. S.* ☎ *206/682-9697; 400 Pine St.* ☎ *206/682-6462. www.fireworks gallery.net. AE, MC, V. Bus: 15, 18, 21, 22, 56. Map p 80.*

Kobo CAPITOL HILL   Beautiful Northwest and Asian products are the focus here: pottery, teas, unusual gifts, and travel items. *814 E. Roy St.* ☎ *206/726-0704. www.koboseattle.com. AE, DISC, MC, V. Bus: 49. Map p 82.*

★★ kids **Lanna Trading Co.** PIONEER SQUARE   For the friend who has everything, head to this small shop and pick up some elephant art. That's right, colorful canvases by pachyderm painters. If you

don't believe it, watch the DVD of Thai elephants at their craft. The owner also stocks a great assortment of other items that he personally shops for in Thailand, and there's something for every budget. *87 Yesler Way.* ☎ *206/262-9798. www.lannaimports.com. AE, MC, V. Bus: 16, 99. Map p 80.*

★★ **Made in Washington** PIKE PLACE MARKET   This is no tacky souvenir shop: Take something home to your friends from Made in Washington and it's guaranteed not to end up at their garage sale. Plus, the store is just plain fun, and offers a wide range of prices. *400 Pine St.* ☎ *206/623-9753. Downtown location: 1530 Post Alley.* ☎ *206/467-0788. www.madeinwashington.com. AE, DISC, MC, V. Bus: 15, 18, 21, 22, 56. Map p 81.*

Merry Tails PIONEER SQUARE   This is a great place to find a souvenir for Fido, or for any pet-lover on your list. There are lots of breed-specific items and unusual gifts. *1409 1st*

Fireworks offers one-stop shopping for all of those items you don't really need but really, really want.

KOBO

An artisan gallery featuring fine crafts and design from Japan and the Northwest

KOBO Capitol Hill
814 East Roy Street
Seattle, WA 98102
(206) 726-0704

KOBO at Higo
International District
604 S. Jackson Street
Seattle, WA 98104
(206) 381-3000
info@koboseattle.com

Stock up on gifts you won't find anywhere else at Kobo.

Ave. ☎ 206/623-4142. Bus: 15, 18, 21, 22, 56. Map p 81.

★★★ Millstream DOWNTOWN I always feel like I'm stepping into a mountain cabin when I enter this woodsy-themed shop at Westlake Center. But you won't find kitsch here. The talents of many serious Pacific Northwest artists are showcased here. You can buy jewelry crafted from British Columbia jade, woodcarvings from Alaska, soapstone figurines by local Native American tribes, and many other unusual handmade items. *400 Pine St., Ste. 118.* ☎ *206/233-9719. www.millstreamseattle.com. AE, MC, V. Bus: 11, 12, 49. Map p 79.*

★ Noble Horse Gallery PIONEER SQUARE True to its name, this unusual shop is filled with every horse item imaginable—and quite a few you'd never think of. You can buy equestrian-themed art, clothes, books, and home decor, including horse-shaped shower hooks. And yes, you can buy a saddle here. *216 1st Ave. S., Ste. G07.* ☎ *206/382-8566. www.noblehorsegallery.com. AE, DISC, MC, V. Bus: 15, 18, 21, 22, 56. Map p 80.*

kids Pirates Plunder WATERFRONT This is the place to go for all things pirate! Seriously, this shop specializes in pirate-related booty ranging from T-shirts to artwork. *www.piratesplunder.com. AE, DISC, MC, V. Bus: 99. Map p 79.*

★★★ Twist DOWNTOWN This fun Northwest store, located in Pacific Place shopping mall, is bursting with color. Feast your eyes on the whimsical hand-carved furniture, avantgarde art jewelry, and beautiful glassware. You'll find lots of upscale gifts here, plus a few unique items that won't strain your budget. *600 Pine St., Ste. 130.* ☎ *206/315-8080. www.twistonline.com. AE, DISC, MC, V. Bus: 11, 12, 49. Map p 79.*

Glass

★★★ Foster/White PIONEER SQUARE This gallery, housed in a century-old building, is more than glass; you'll also find contemporary paintings and sculptures by premier artists. But one of its main claims to fame is representing world-famous glass artist Dale Chihuly. You can always find works by the master here. *220 3rd Ave. S.* ☎ *206/622-2833;*

Ahoy matey! A wooden pirate keeps an eye on Pirates Plunder.

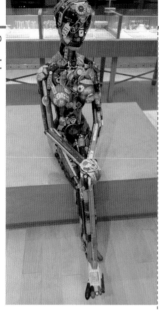

One of the unique displays at Twist (p 89).

1331 5th Ave. ☎ 206/622-2833. www.fosterwhite.com. AE, MC, V. Bus: 358. Map p 80.

★★★ kids **Glasshouse Studio**
PIONEER SQUARE   In addition to being a working artists' studio, Glasshouse sells the wares of many local glass artists. The shelves here are bursting with color. You can buy everything from a simple vase to a huge chandelier shaped like an exuberant explosion of peppers. 311 Occidental Ave. S. ☎ 206/682-9939. www.glasshouse-studio.com. AE, DISC, MC, V. Bus: 99. Map p 80.

★★★ kids **Seattle Glassblowing Studio** DOWNTOWN   The studio offers classes in glassblowing, and the gallery features fanciful work by a variety of artists. Be sure to check out the colorful glass art sinks. The studio is open to the public, so you can watch the artists at work. 2227 5th Ave. ☎ 206/448-2181. www.seattle glassblowing.com. AE, DISC, MC, V. Bus: 26, 28. Map p 79.

Housewares
★ **City Kitchens** DOWNTOWN
Think kitchen stores are boring? You haven't seen this one. The shelves are filled with every gadget imaginable, plus products for the demanding cook ranging from Cuisinart cookware to fine knives. Don't miss the close-out room off to the side. 1527 4th Ave. ☎ 206/382-1138. AE, DISC, MC, V. Bus: 10. Map p 79.

★ **Sur La Table** PIONEER SQUARE
Everything at this store inspires even a mediocre cook like myself to go home and put on an apron. Better yet, pick one out from Sur La Table's beautiful selection of kitchen and dining linens. They have everything from ceramic cookware to oven mitts, but my favorite section is the exotic oils and spices. 84 Pine St. ☎ 206/448-2244. www.surlatable.com. AE, DISC, MC, V. Bus: 15, 18, 21, 22, 56. Map p 81.

Malls
★ **Pacific Place** DOWNTOWN
This elegant upscale mall is a great place for shopping, if your budget allows, but also fun for just browsing. See p 62. 6th Ave & Pine St. ☎ 206/405-2655. www.pacificplaceseattle.com. Bus: 11, 12, 49. Map p 79.

★★ **Westlake Center** DOWNTOWN   This is usually where I go when I actually want to buy something at a mall. Lots of clothing and gift stores, with items at just about any price. See p 63. 400 Pine St. ☎ 206/467-1600. www.westlake center.com. Bus: 11, 12, 49. Map p 79.

Music/CDs
★★ **Easy Street Records and CDs** QUEEN ANNE   This roomy store is a music-lover's nirvana, offering a vast inventory of CDs and vinyl, and even in-store concerts (check the website). Private listening stations are scattered throughout the store, and

you can even buy unusual musical gift items. *20 Mercer St.* ☎ *206/691-3279. www.buymusichere.net/stores/easystreet/enter.html. MC, V. Bus: 1, 2, 13, 15, 18. Map p 79.*

★★ kids Lark in the Morning Musique Shoppe PIKE PLACE MARKET   This is a delightful place to spend a spare hour, even if you're not in the market for a harp, guitar, dulcimer, tambourine, accordion, crystal flute, or any of the other beautifully crafted instruments for sale here. Even if you can't play a note, it's fun to try them out. *1401 1st Ave.* ☎ *206/623-3440. www.larkinthemorning.com. Bus: 15, 18, 21, 22, 56. Map p 81.*

★★ Silver Platters QUEEN ANNE   Odds are you'll be able to find that obscure CD at this spacious independent music shop, whether you're into punk or jazz. The staff is very knowledgeable, and you can listen to most of the music before you buy. They also have a great movie selection on DVD. *701 5th Ave. N.* ☎ *206/283-3472. www.silverplatters.com. MC, V. Bus: 10. Map p 79.*

★★ Wall of Sound CAPITOL HILL   This eclectic shop specializes in international, avant-garde, electronic, and experimental music, and you'll also find a great selection of mainstream CDs. Check the website for visiting artists and indie movie screenings. *315 E. Pine St.* ☎ *206/441-9880. www.wosound.com. MC, V. Bus: 43. Map p 82.*

Perfume/Skincare/
Herbal Products
Lush Cosmetics DOWNTOWN   Who would have thought soap could be so much fun? You can suds yourself in just about any scent your heart desires. If you like, pick a sparkly bar, with glitter that lasts as long as the soap. With such an affordable, beautiful product, this is one of the most popular shops at Westlake Center. *400 Pine St., Ste. 100.* ☎ *206/624-5874. www.lush.com. AE, DISC, MC, V. Bus: 11, 12, 49. Map p 79.*

Pelindaba Lavender Gallery DOWNTOWN   The home decor, personal care, and culinary items in this lovely little shop are made from lavender grown on the Pelindaba Lavender farm on San Juan Island in Western Washington. *1420 5th Ave.* ☎ *206/264-0508. www.pelindaba lavender.com. AE, MC, V. Bus: 10. Map p 79.*

Seattle Soapworks PIONEER SQUARE   Just walking into this shop is a relaxing experience. The aromas of lavender body wash, Italian soaps, botanical candles—even tea bags for the bathtub—waft through the doorway. *157 S. Jackson St.* ☎ *206/223-2222. www.seattle soapworks.com. AE, DISC, MC, V. Bus: 99. Map p 80.*

Tenzing Momo & Company PIKE PLACE MARKET   This little shop will meet all your New Age needs: aromatherapy oils and books, incense, herbs, and tarot cards. *93 Pike St., Ste. 203.* ☎ *206/623-9837. www.tenzingmomo.com. AE, DISC, MC, V. Bus: 15, 18, 21, 22, 56. Map p 81.*

If you don't have time to visit the San Juan Islands, at least stock up on the area's finest lavender at Pelindaba Lavender Gallery.

Pets
Mud Bay Granary CAPITOL HILL The pet food is natural and healthy, and you'll find every accessory a well-heeled doggy—or feline—could dream of. *815 E. Thomas St.* ☎ *206/322-6177. www.mudbay.us. AE, DISC, MC, V. Bus: 49. Map p 82.*

Rugs
Golden Loom Rug Gallery PIONEER SQUARE Beautiful, high-quality floor coverings in all colors and patterns are available at this store in the "rug district" of Pioneer Square. *211 1st Ave. S.* ☎ *206/903-8286. AE, DISC, MC, V. Bus: 15, 18, 21, 22, 56. Map p 80.*

★ **Palace Rug Gallery** PIONEER SQUARE Colorful wool and silk rugs from Afghanistan, Pakistan, and China are stacked high in this large space. They are all handmade, and some take up to 16 months to complete. Not sure if it will work in your home? If you're local, you can take several home and try them out. *323 1st Ave. S.* ☎ *206/382-7401. www.palacerug.com. AE, DISC, MC, V. Bus: 15, 18, 21, 22, 56. Map p 80.*

Shoes
★ **The Clog Factory** PIONEER SQUARE Talk about a niche! If you're in the market for clogs, this is definitely the place to go. They've

The Clog Factory specializes in—what else?—clogs.

got them in all colors, shapes, and sizes, from Mary Janes to slippers. *217 1st Ave. S.* ☎ *206/682-2564. AE, DISC, MC, V. Bus: 15, 18, 21, 22, 56. Map p 80.*

kids **Niketown.** DOWNTOWN You'll find all the latest Nike shoes here, and lots of tributes to the top athletes who endorse them. *1500 6th Ave.* ☎ *206/447-6453. www. niketown5k.com. AE, MC, V. Bus: 11, 12, 49. Map p 79.*

Toys & Novelties
★ **kids** **Dragon's Toy Box** PIKE PLACE MARKET From chemistry sets to puppets, the shelves here are filled with quality toys and learning aids. *1525 1st Ave., Ste. 2A.* ☎ *206/652-2333. www.dragonstoy box.com. AE, MC, V. Bus: 15, 18, 21, 22, 56. Map p 81.*

★★ **kids** **Magic Mouse Toys** PIONEER SQUARE I have as hard a time as my 9-year-old daughter tearing myself away from this wonderful, multi-level toy store. These are real toys, the kind built to last. There are lots of learning-focused books, games, and kits, and an entire room dedicated to puzzles. Adults will enjoy reminiscing and laughing at the political novelty items. And everyone is encouraged to play. *603 1st Ave.* ☎ *206/682-8097. AE, MC, V. Bus: 15, 18, 21, 22, 56. Map p 80.*

★★ **kids** **Market Magic & Novelty Shop** PIONEER SQUARE Making magic for 30 years, this store buried deep in the Market has been visited by a number of well-known magicians over the years. There's usually some sleight-of-hand in progress; just look for the row of gawking kids. Beginning and experienced tricksters will find props, books, and DVDs galore. *1501 Pike Place #427.* ☎ *206/624-4271. AE, MC, V. Bus: 15, 18, 21, 22, 56. Map p 81.* ●

5 The Best of the **Outdoors**

94

The Best of the Outdoors

The Seattle **Waterfront**

1 Victor Steinbrueck Park
2 Odyssey Maritime Discovery Center
3 Cruise Terminal
4 Seattle Aquarium
5 Waterfront Park
6 Bay Pavilion
7 Argosy Cruises
8 Ivar's Seafood Bar
9 Washington State Ferry Terminal

If there's one thing that rivals mountains in the hearts of Pacific Northwesterners, it's water. At the Seattle waterfront—on a clear day—you get both. The Olympics form a jaggedly endearing backdrop to sparkling Elliott Bay. Add a few gleaming white ferryboats crisscrossing their way over the Puget Sound, and your souvenir snapshot is waiting. This is a lively place to spend the day—though noisy, thanks to the traffic rushing along an elevated highway across from the waterfront. START: **Waterfront Streetcar Line (Bus 99).**

❶ Victor Steinbrueck Park. Just north of Pike Place Market, toward the Bay, lies a waterfront park named for a local architect who helped spearhead the efforts to preserve Pike Place Market. It's a great place for a picnic or people-watching. If the weather gods are with you, you'll be treated to a panoramic view of mountains—the Cascades (starring Mount Rainier) curving around to the east and the Olympics to the west. Just be aware that panhandlers are frequent guests here, too. *2001 Western Ave. Daily 6am–11:30pm.*

❷ kids Odyssey Maritime Discovery Center. Paddle a virtual kayak. Learn to identify the many types of vessels you can spot in the Puget Sound. Find out how goods move back and forth between Seattle and Asia. This unusual museum gives a nuts-and-bolts perspective of the link between the Pacific Northwest and the waters that surround it. The displays are interactive, with lots of buttons to press and activities to try. Kids love it, but you'll likely see just as many adults trying to "steer" the container ship. *2205 Alaskan Way, Pier 66. ☎ 206/374-4000. $7 adults, $5 seniors & ages 5–18, $2 ages 2–4, free for kids under 2. Wed–Thurs 10am–3pm; Fri 10am–4pm; Sat–Sun 11am–5pm.*

❸ Cruise Terminal. Seattle is a great hopping-off point for cruises to Alaska, and that's where most of the luxury cruise ships you'll see here are headed. Three- and 4-day cruises to British Columbia are also available. Five major cruise lines come and go from this port: Celebrity, Holland America, Norwegian, Princess, and Royal Caribbean. The cruise schedule is available at the Port of Seattle's website. I always get a kick out of watching the enormous floating hotels

A statue of Christopher Columbus graces Waterfront Park (p 96).

Seattle Celebrates Summer

When the winters are as long and gray as they are in Seattle, who can blame the locals for going a little nuts when summer shows up, with its picture-perfect days that stretch until 10 at night? Getting a jump on the season is the Northwest Folklife Festival, held at Seattle Center in May and showcasing the region's cultures. In June, the Seattle Pride Festival celebrates the gay community. At Bite of Seattle in late June, crowds elbow their way into Seattle Center to hear live bands and sample gourmet treats and wine from local restaurants. Summer is officially kicked off by the Fourth of July fireworks over Lake Union—among the finest displays in the nation—and also over beautiful Elliott Bay. Seafair is a month of parades, competitions, and hydroplane races celebrating pirates and everything aquatic. The mother of all festivals, Bumbershoot, marks the end of summer and return of the drizzle. Fine arts, crafts, acrobats, big-name bands, and general zaniness rule supreme at Seattle Center over the Labor Day weekend.

come and go. *2225 Alaskan Way S.* ☎ *206/615-3900. www.portseattle. org/seaport/cruise.*

④ ★★ kids **Seattle Aquarium.** This excellent aquarium recently underwent a $41 million expansion, and it shows. One of the new exhibits is the Window on Washington Waters, which takes a look at local marine life. And keep an eye out for the always adorable sea otters—they tend to steal the show. *1483 Alaskan Way Pier 59.* ☎ *206/386-4300. www.seattle aquarium.org. Admission $15 adults, $10 ages 4–12. Daily 9:30am–5pm. See p 35.*

⑤ **Waterfront Park.** Stretching between Piers 57 and 59, this unconventional park is my favorite spot for watching all the action out in Elliott Bay. It's not a green oasis, but you can't beat the location. With the Waterfront Fountain sculpture splashing merrily in the background, you can peer at your leisure at the

working boats, cruise ships, and the occasional seal. Coin-operated telescopes bring it all into focus. *1301 Alaskan Way.*

⑥ kids **Bay Pavilion.** On a drizzly day, this is a good place to duck out of the rain, browse the fun shops, and let the kids play. It's on Pier 57.

⑦ ★★★ **Argosy Cruises.** In addition to its tours of Elliott Bay and Tillicum Village, Argosy offers brunch, lunch, and dinner cruises; a tour of lakes Washington and Union (including a look at the famous Seattle houseboats); and a cruise through the Hiram Chittenden Locks. There are themed cruises, holiday cruises, musical cruises—you name it, they've got a cruise. ⏱ *1–2½ hr. Pier 55, Seattle Waterfront.* ☎ *206/ 623-1445. www.argosycruises.com.*

⑧ᴾ ★ **Ivar's Seafood Bar.** The best bowl of clam chowder in Seattle, for my money, is right here at Ivar's, which has been dishing out local seafood since 1938. You can also get clams 'n chips, oysters 'n chips, and a variety of other fresh, locally caught treats for munching as you wander the waterfront. Or take a break and relax at one of the outdoor tables set up beside the bar. *Pier 54.* ☎ *206/467-8063. Mon–Thurs 11am–10pm; Fri–Sat 11am–11pm; Sun 9am–10pm.*

Rides on the vintage carousel at Bay Pavilion cost $1.50 per person.

⑨ Washington State Ferry Terminal. From here, you can glide your way to Bainbridge Island, Bremerton, or Vashon Island. For Vashon, this is passenger-only service. For the others, you can walk or take your car, but the latter is pricier, and the lines can be much longer. If you just want to walk onto a ferry, go for a ride, and then poke around town, Bainbridge is your best option. If the weather's nice and you'd like a long, leisurely ride to enjoy the experience, take the hour-long Bremerton run. And if you want to go exploring the Kitsap or Olympic peninsulas (the latter takes you through the rainforest to the northwestern edge of the state), drive onto the Bremerton ferry and leave from that side of the Sound.

Stop into Ivar's and try the excellent clam chowder.

Hiram J. Chittenden Locks

① Visitors Center
② Carl S. English, Jr. Botanical Garden
③ Fish Ladder
④ Hiram J. Chittenden Locks
⑤ Lockspot Café

Watching the boats navigate the locks is a fascinating enough way to spend an afternoon, but at Hiram J. Chittenden, there's much more: those amazing climbing fish, the painstakingly tended botanical gardens, and the best grassy hills in town for kids to roll down. (Do keep an eye out for goose droppings.) You'll also find lots of prime picnic spots where you can munch as you watch the boats go by. START: **3015 NW 54th St.**

① **Visitors Center.** Stop here first for free brochures of the locks and gardens, and watch the informational video shown every half-hour. The staff is happy to answer questions. Free hour-long guided tours are offered from March 1–Nov 30 (weekdays 1 and 3pm; Sat–Sun 2pm). *3015 NW 54th St.* ☎ *206/783-7059. May 1–Sept 30 daily 10am–4pm; Oct 1–Apr 30 Thurs–Mon 10am–4pm.*

② **Carl S. English, Jr. Botanical Garden.** Building and dredging the

Come watch the salmon head upstream with little help from human technology at the Fish Ladder.

The Botanical Garden is one of Seattle's hidden gems.

steelhead salmon. You can watch them climbing the ladders outdoors, then head down to an underwater viewing room. Though it's open year-round, you likely won't find much but water October to May. *3015 NW 54th St.* ☎ *206/783-7059. Daily 7am–9pm.*

④ kids **Hiram J. Chittenden Locks.** I never tire of watching boats of all shapes and sizes make their ascent from the Puget Sound up into Lake Washington. Some pretty magnificent yachts come through here. If you're lucky, you might spot one of billionaire Paul Allen's mega-yachts. They're hard to miss. *3015 NW 54th St.* ☎ *206/783-7059. Daily 7am–9pm.*

⑤ **Lockspot Café.** You can't miss this eatery at the entrance to the locks: Just look for the undersea mural, complete with mermaid and orca. Grab some fish and chips at the outside counter and have a picnic at the locks. You can also dine inside in a publike atmosphere, but if it's a nice day, I'd opt for the picnic. *3005 NW 54th St.* ☎ *206/789-4865. Mon–Fri 11am–2am; Sat–Sun 8am–2am.*

The Lockspot Cafe is a perfect place for a seafood break.

locks produced a vast amount of empty space. Botanist Carl S. English, Jr. came to the rescue, transforming the grounds into a splendid English-style garden with plants from around the globe. This fragrant, blooming quilt is a much-treasured Seattle secret. *3015 NW 54th St.* ☎ *206/783-7059. Daily 7am–9pm.*

③ ★★ **Fish Ladder.** Salmon have got to be the most inspirational fish around. They hatch in streams, swim out to the ocean, then years later they fight their way back upstream, to their exact birthplace, to start the cycle again. Here, they swim from the ocean into the Puget Sound, climb a 21-"step" ladder to get up to freshwater Lake Washington level, then head home. It takes a lot of energy for a salmon to swim and flop its way up the ladder, but persistence pays. At different times during the summer you might see sockeye, Chinook, coho, and

Green Lake Park

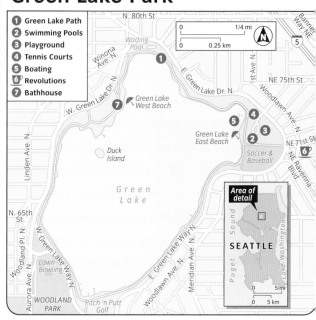

1 Green Lake Path
2 Swimming Pools
3 Playground
4 Tennis Courts
5 Boating
6 Revolutions
7 Bathhouse

Rain or shine, the locals grab their dogs and head here for their daily dose of fresh air. The path, nearly 3 miles (5km) long, winds around a beautiful glacier-carved lake, ringed by spectacular trees and Northwest plants. Cars zoom past on busy State Road 99, but the highway is just far enough away from this green oasis that you barely notice. START: **7201 E. Green Lake Dr. N.**

1 **★★ Green Lake Path.** The trail is separated into a crushed granite inner lane for walkers, joggers, and strollers; and an outer asphalt lane for bicyclists and skaters. Added bonus: The bird-watching is great! *7201 E. Green Lake Dr. N.*

2 **kids Swimming Pools.** In addition to the outdoor wading pool and indoor heated pool, there is a beach on the lakefront with life-guards and diving boards in the summertime. However, Green Lake

has frequent algae blooms when the weather turns warm, so check for informational signs before you go for a dip. *See p 37, bullet* 8.

3 **★ kids Playground.** Parents and kids alike can take a break at this terrific play area, which offers some cool features not found in other parks. My daughter's favorite was always the sand pit with the sand-digging machine and the canoe for imaginary trips. If the weather turns nasty, the park's

Strolling the Green Lake Path affords excellent views of the surrounding area.

nearby community center has an indoor playroom for the younger set. *E. Green Lake Way & Latona Ave. NE (near the main entrance).*

4 Tennis Courts. You'll find some just inside the main entrance, at 7201 E. Green Lake Dr. N., and also at W. Greenlake Way and Stone Ave. N. *To reserve a court, call* ☎ *206/684-4075.*

5 Boating. Take a canoe out on the lake—or a kayak or a paddle boat. You can rent them north of the main entrance and launch from there or the regular boat launch on the southwest side of the lake. *7351 E. Green Lake Dr. N.* ☎ *206/527-0171.*

6 Revolutions. Fresh-baked goods are made on site, and the coffee comes from Caffe Vita Coffee Roasting Co. of Seattle. *7012 Woodlawn Ave. NE.* ☎ *206/ 527-1908. Mon–Fri 6am–10pm; Sat–Sun 7am–9pm.*

7 ★ Bathhouse. This former bathhouse from the 1920s has been converted into a popular playhouse on the west wide of the lake. There, tucked away in the middle of Green Lake Park, Seattle Public Theater presents often-controversial works that are usually worth seeing. *7312 W. Greenlake Dr. N.* ☎ *206/524-1300. www.seattlepublictheater.org.*

Take a boat out on the lake, just like the locals do.

Washington Park Arboretum

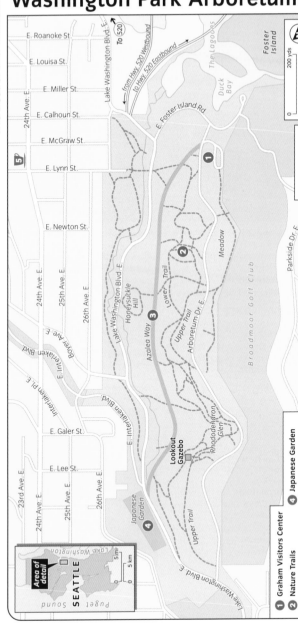

E. Roanoke St.

E. Louisa St.

E. Miller St.

E. Calhoun St.

E. McGraw St.

E. Lynn St.

E. Newton St.

E. Galer St.

E. Lee St.

24th Ave. E.

25th Ave. E.

26th Ave. E.

23rd Ave. E.

24th Ave. E.

25th Ave. E.

26th Ave. E.

Boyer Ave. E.

E. Interlaken Blvd.

Interlaken Pl. E.

Lake Washington Blvd. E.

from Hwy 520 Westbound

to Hwy 520 Eastbound

To 520

E. Foster Island Rd.

The Lagoons

Foster Island

Duck Bay

Meadow

Broadmoor Golf Club

Parkside Dr. E.

Honeysuckle Hill

Azalea Way

Lower Trail

Upper Trail

Arboretum Dr. E.

Rhododendron Glen

Lookout Gazebo

Japanese Garden

Upper Trail

Lake Washington Blvd. E.

200 yds

200 m

- - - - - Walking trail

1 Graham Visitors Center
2 Nature Trails
3 Azalea Way
4 Japanese Garden
5 Montlake Ale House

Area of detail

SEATTLE

Lake Washington

Puget Sound

5 mi

5 km

This is Seattle's garden, sprawled along 200 acres (80 hectares) of lush property, with Lake Washington winding its way around the northern edge of the park. Breathtaking any time of year, the arboretum is especially stunning in the spring and early summer. Thousands of exotic plants have been gathered from every corner of the world—75 countries, to be exact. START: Bus 11, 43, or 48 to McGraw St.

Get lost in a sea of color along Azalea Way.

1 Graham Visitors Center. Stop here for a map of the trails, then wander among the trees, ponds, and shrubs of the Arboretum (open daily dawn–dusk) at your leisure. *2300 Arboretum Dr.* ☎ *206/ 543-8800. Daily 10am–4pm.*

2 ★★ kids Nature Trails. Pick a trail—any trail—and start hiking! It's a good idea to bring along a light backpack for snacks and water. These trails are all easy walks, with no hills to scale. My favorite is the Foster Island trail, which winds along a boardwalk through an emerald-green wetland area, and leads to two islands. You'll be rewarded with spectacular views over Lake Washington.

3 Azalea Way. This garden near Graham Visitors Center comes alive in the springtime, when it is a ¾-mile (1.2km) promenade of riotous azaleas and cherry blossoms. *2300 Arboretum Dr.*

4 ★★★ Japanese Garden. The centerpiece of the Arboretum, this exquisite garden is where I come when I need to unwind. It's the perfect place to sit and contemplate life. World-famous Japanese garden artist Juki Iida designed it with nearly divine grace and beauty. Formal tea ceremonies are held occasionally at the Shoseian Teahouse inside the garden (check the Urasenke Foundation's website for dates and times: http://urasenke seattle.org). *1075 Lake Washington Blvd. E.* ☎ *206/684-4725. $5 adults, $3 seniors & ages 6–17, free for children under 6. Open Mar–Nov daily 10am–dusk.*

5 Montlake Ale House. You can bring the kids along to this friendly pub, where a dining bar surrounds a sunken play area filled with toys. It's nice to be able to relax with a pint and a plate of tortilla chips and guacamole with the kiddies safely confined. *2307 24th Ave. E.* ☎ *206/726-5968.*

The best time to visit is in the spring, when everything is in bloom, but the arboretum is gorgeous year-round.

Woodland Park

1 Woodland Park Zoo
2 Woodland Park Rose Garden
3 ZooTunes
4 Woodland Park

The focal point, of course, is the **Woodland Park Zoo,** a must-see stop for families with kids. It's surrounded by grassy hills that are perfect for picnics and afternoons of fun. The part west of Highway 99 (Aurora Ave.) is occupied mainly by the zoo; to the east of the highway stretch the parklands, which adjoin Green Lake Park. START: **Bus 16 or 44.**

1 ★★★ kids **Woodland Park Zoo.** There's never a dull moment at the Woodland Park Zoo, where the tenants range from red pandas to vampire bats. In 2007, the zoo saw the birth of a western lowland gorilla and the first birthday of an endangered Sumatran tiger cub, also born there. Though a zoo of some sort has occupied Woodland Park since the 1890s, the animal habitats at the present-day facility are the cutting edge of zoo technology. 🕑 *2 hr. 750 N. 50th St.* ☎ *206/684-4800.*

www.zoo.org. Admission May–Sept $15 ages 13–64, $10 ages 3–12; Oct– Apr $11 ages 13–64, $8 ages 3–12. May–Sept daily 9:30am–6pm; Oct– Apr daily 9:30am–4pm. See p 37.

2 ★★ **Woodland Park Rose Garden.** Roses love the Pacific Northwest, and even non-flower- lovers will be captivated by the beauty and diversity packed into this 2½-acre (1-hectare) garden. One of only 24 All-America Rose Selec- tions test sites in the country, the

Come visit the local fauna, such as grizzly bears, along with more exotic species, at the Woodland Park Zoo.

3 ★★ ZooTunes. Summertime means outdoor concert season at Woodland Park Zoo, and they're always great fun. I've seen acts as time-honored as Art Garfunkel and as hip as Pink Martini. Bring a blanket or a low beach chair—yours will actually be measured if it looks too tall—and settle in the meadow, just inside the zoo's north entrance. Kids are welcome and dancing is encouraged! If you plan to visit Seattle from mid-June through August, check the schedule (www.zoo.org/zootunes) in early May. If you see a concert you like, book early because they sell out fast. The website explains how to buy tickets over the Internet. The prices are quite reasonable compared to most venues, averaging around $21 a ticket, plus a service fee for Web sales. *N. 59th & Evanston Ave.* ☎ *206/615-0076.*

Woodland Park Rose Garden displays the very latest varieties. It's no wonder the garden is always in great demand for weddings. You'll find it east of the zoo's south entrance gate, but in the summertime your nose will lead you there. *700 N. 50th St. Free admission. Daily 7am–dusk.*

4 Woodland Park. This large urban park is a favorite picnic spot. Sheltered areas hold from 50 to 300 people, and these may be rented starting at $40 per day. You'll also find tennis courts, horseshoes, a ball field, playground, and an off-leash dog area. *Aurora Ave. N. & N. 59th St.* ☎ *206/684-4081.*

The Woodland Park Rose Garden.

Seattle Center

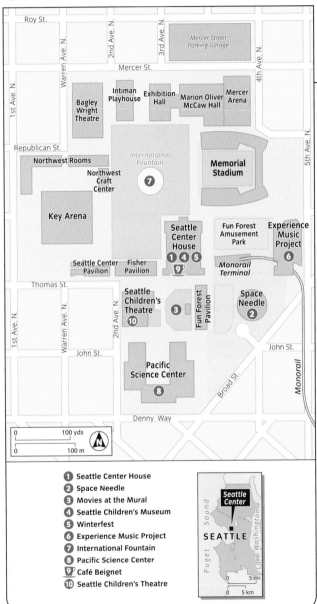

1. Seattle Center House
2. Space Needle
3. Movies at the Mural
4. Seattle Children's Museum
5. Winterfest
6. Experience Music Project
7. International Fountain
8. Pacific Science Center
9. Café Beignet
10. Seattle Children's Theatre

This is where Seattle comes to party. From the spectacular
fountain—where Northwesterners "cool off" as soon as it hits
the 60s—to the myriad of festivals that mark summertime in Seattle,
there's always fun to be had here. Even in the winter, the grounds
are a lovely place to enjoy a book on a sunny day. If it gets too chilly,
I usually pop into the Center House for hot chocolate. START: **Monorail
or bus 1, 2, 3, 4, 13, 15, 16, 17, or 18 to Seattle Center.**

❶ ★ Seattle Center House.
This huge building is a focal point for
every Seattle Center event, with
indoor activities that go hand-in-hand
with the festivities. And in Seattle, it's
important to have a large space for
crowds to gather when the raindrops
start to fall. Even during the rare
times when there's no festival in
progress, Seattle Center often hosts
art shows and cultural activities, and
frequently has musical performances
stage. The inside perimeter is lined
with restaurants, cafes, and a candy
shop (p 85).

❷ ★★★ Space Needle. Take a
ride to the top and, on a clear day,
you'll see all of Seattle (and Mt.
Rainier) at your feet. ⏱ *1 hr. Summer
weekends are busiest. 400 Broad St.*
☎ *206/905-2180. www.space
needle.com. Observation deck tickets
$16 adults, $14 seniors, $8 ages
4–13. Sun–Thurs 9am–11pm; Fri–Sat
9am–noon. See p 48,* ⓮.

❸ Movies at the Mural. Every
August weekend, families bring their
blankets and folding chairs (low,
please) to the Mural Amphitheatre,
to lounge on the lawn and watch a
movie projected onto a giant
screen. Outdoor cinema on a perfect Seattle evening with the Space
Needle as a backdrop—what could
be better? Check the website for the
schedule (www.seattlecenter.com,
click on "Seattle Center Programs").

**❹ ★ kids Seattle Children's
Museum.** Stop in and let the kids

run wild. ⏱ *90 min. 305 Harrison St.*
☎ *206/441-1768. www.thechildrens
museum.org. Admission $7.50 adults
& children, free for kids under age 1.
Mon–Fri 10am–5pm; Sat–Sun 10am–
6pm. See p 36,* ❹.

❺ ★ Winterfest. Starting Thanksgiving weekend and running through
December, this celebration puts a little magic in the cold season. A huge
train set, complete with an oversized
turn-of-the-century village, takes up
much of the Center House, and for a
small donation kids can take a turn
at the switcher that operates the
train (10am–6:30pm). Choirs, bon-
fires, ice sculpting, and storytelling
are just part of the fun. Fisher Pavilion, just outside the Center House, is
turned into an ice rink (Sun–Thurs
11am–8pm, Fri–Sat 11am–10pm; $5

*Yes, it's indoors, but the Experience Music
Project (p 108) shouldn't be missed.*

adults, $3 ages 6–12) and is kept open through the first weekend of January. An antique carousel just outside the pavilion is open the same hours; rides are just $1.

6 ★ Experience Music Project. This is the house that Jimi built—sort of. Microsoft co-founder Paul Allen combined his love of rock music (and, specifically, the music of Seattle-born guitar god Jimi Hendrix) and futuristic architecture and came up with EMP. It's got both permanent and rotating exhibits. ⏱ *30 min. 1000 4th Ave.* ☎ *206/386-4636. www.spl. org. Free admission. Mon–Thurs 10am–8pm; Fri–Sat 10am–6pm; Sun noon–6pm. See p 47,* **13**.

7 ★ International Fountain. It's hard to match Seattle on a summer day for sheer joy, and you'll see plenty of it expressed at this colossal fountain just north of the Center House. Kids, grown-ups, and a dog or two charge down the concrete ramp to splash through a glorious spray of playful water. Sunbathers arrange themselves around the fountain to soak up the rays. At night, the waters dance to rainbow colors.

8 ★★ kids Pacific Science Center. This Seattle institution offers a hands-on approach to science that's fun for everyone. ⏱ *2 hr. 200 2nd Ave. N.* ☎ *206/443-2844. www.pacsci.org. Admission $11 adults, $9.50 seniors, $8 ages 6–12, $6 ages 3–5. IMAX $8–$11 adults, $7.50–$9.50 seniors, $7–$8.50 ages 6–12, $6 ages 3–5, discounts available for combination passes. Mon–Fri 10am–5pm; Sat–Sun 10am–6pm. See p 36,* **6**.

9 ★ Café Beignet. The fried dough treats may not be exactly like you'd find in New Orleans, but they are nevertheless light, sweet, and delicious. Unless you're neater than me, be prepared to be covered in powdered sugar. I strongly recommend washing them down with a mocha latte, one of the best in town. *Center House.* ☎ *206/441-0262. Sun–Thurs 7am–6pm; Fri–Sat 7am–8pm.*

10 ★★★ kids Seattle Children's Theatre. This kid-friendly performance center offers shows that will entertain the whole family. *201 Thomas St., at Seattle Center.* ☎ *206/ 441-3322. www.sct.org. Ticket prices vary. See p 35,* **2**. ●

The International Fountain is the perfect place to cool down on a hot summer day— go ahead and splash away.

Dining **Best Bets**

Best **French Cuisine**
★★★ Campagne, 86 Pine St. $$$$
(p115)

Best **Brunch**
★★ Salty's on Alki, 1936 Harbor
Ave. SW. $$$ (p 122)

Best **Salmon**
★★ Etta's Seafood, 2020 Western
Ave. $$$ (p 117)

Best **Special Occasion**
★★★ Canlis, 2576 Aurora Ave. N.
$$$$ (p 116)

Best **Steak**
★★★ Metropolitan Grill, 820 2nd
Ave. $$$$ (p 120)

Most **Classic Style & Service**
★★ Morton's, 1511 6th Ave. $$$$
(p 120)

Best **Waterfront Dining**
★★ Palisade, 2601 W. Marina Place
$$$–$$$$ (p 121)

Best for **Vegetarians**
★★ Typhoon!, 1400 Western Ave.
$$ (p 123); and ★★ Wild Ginger,
1401 3rd Ave. $$–$$$ (p 124)

Best **Dim Sum**
★★ China Gate, 516 7th Ave. S.
$–$$ (p 116)

Best **Hotel Fine Dining**
★★★ Hunt Club, 900 Madison St.
$$$ (p 118)

Best **Pre-Theater**
★★ Tulio Ristorante, 2323 2nd Ave.
$$$ (p 123)

Best **Pre-Opera (or Pre-Basketball Game)**
★★ Moxie, 530 1st Ave. N. $$$
(p 120)

Best **Sushi**
★★ Shiro's, 2401 2nd Ave. $$ (p 122)

Most **Fun with Friends**
★★ Assaggio, 2010 4th Ave. $$–$$$
(p 115)

Best **Entertainment While
You Eat**
★★ The Pink Door, 1919 Post Alley
$$–$$$ (p 121)

Best **Late-Night Fine Dining**
★★ Tavolata, 2323 2nd Ave. $$$
(p 123)

Best **Oysters**
★★ Elliott's Oyster House, 1201
Alaskan Way $$$ (p 117)

Best **Outdoor Dining**
★★ McCormick & Schmick's, 1200
Westlake Ave. N. $$$ (p 119)

Best **Lunch**
★★ Marazul, 2200 Westlake Ave. $$
(p 119); and ★★ Le Pichet, 1933 1st
Ave. $$ (p 119)

Hottest **New Bistro**
★★ Steelhead Diner, 5 Pine St.
$$–$$$ (p 123)

Best **Italian Menu**
★★ Il Fornaio, 600 Pine St., Ste. 132
$$–$$$ (p 118)

Salty's is a shellfish lovers dream come true.

Downtown Dining

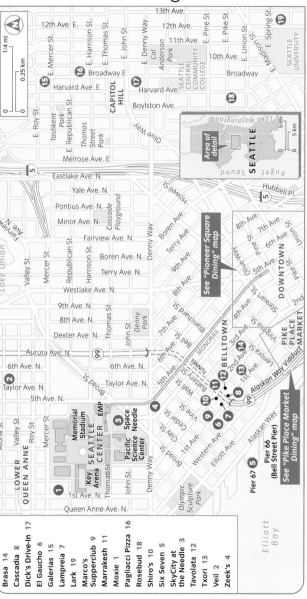

1/4 mi

0.25 km

13th Ave.

12th Ave. E.   12th Ave.   E. Pine St.   E. Pike St.   E. Spring St.

E. Mercer St.   E. Harrison St.   E. Thomas St.   E. John St.   E. Denny Way   11th Ave.   10th Ave.   E. Union St.   E. Madison St.   SEATTLE UNIVERSITY

Cal Anderson Park   SEATTLE CENTRAL COMMUNITY COLLEGE

Broadway E.   Harvard Ave.   Broadway

Harvard Ave. E.   CAPITOL HILL   Boylston Ave.

E. Roy St.   Tashkent Park   E. Republican St.   Thomas Street Park

Olive Way

Melrose Ave. E.

Eastlake Ave. N.

Area of detail   Lake Washington

Puget Sound   SEATTLE   5 mi   5 km

Yale Ave. N.

Pontius Ave. N.   Cascade Playground   Howell St.   Hubbell Pl.

Minor Ave. N.

Fairview Ave. N.   Boren Ave.   8th Ave.   7th Ave.   Union St.

See "Pioneer Square Dining" map   Terry Ave.   6th Ave.   Pike St.

Republican St.   Harrison St.   Boren Ave. N.   9th Ave.

Terry Ave. N.   Stewart St.   5th Ave.   Olive Way

Westlake Ave. N.   DOWNTOWN

Fairview Ave. N.   Valley St.   Mercer St.   Denny Way   Blanchard St.   4th Ave.   Virginia St.   2nd

9th Ave. N.   Thomas St.   Bell St.   PIKE PLACE MARKET

8th Ave. N.   7th Ave.   Battery St.   3rd Ave.

Dexter Ave. N.   Denny Park   Lenora St.   1st Ave.

Aurora Ave. N.   99   John St.   Wall St.   TUNNEL   BELLTOWN   2nd Ave.

6th Ave. N.   6th Ave. N.   Vine St.   MONORAIL   Alaskan Way Viaduct   99

Taylor Ave. N.   Taylor Ave. N.   Cedar St.   Alaskan Way

5th Ave. N.   Clay St.   1st Ave.   Western Ave.   Elliott Ave.

Broad St.   Memorial Stadium   EMP   Space Needle   Pacific Science Center   SEATTLE CENTER   Broad St.

Key Arena   John St.   Denny Way   Pier 67

Aurora   Valley St.   Roy St.   Pier 66 (Bell Street Pier)   See "Pike Place Market Dining" map

LOWER QUEEN ANNE   Mercer St.   Olympic Sculpture Park

1st Ave. N.   Thomas St.

Queen Anne Ave. N.   Elliott Bay

Brasa 14

Cascadia 8

Dick's Drive-In 17

El Gaucho 6

Galeries 15

Lampreia 7

Lark 19

Marco's Supperclub 9

Marrakesh 11

Moxie 1

Pagliacci Pizza 16

Rosebud 18

Shiro's 10

Six Seven 5

SkyCity at the Needle 3

Tavolata 12

Txori 13

Veil 2

Zeek's 4

Pioneer Square Dining

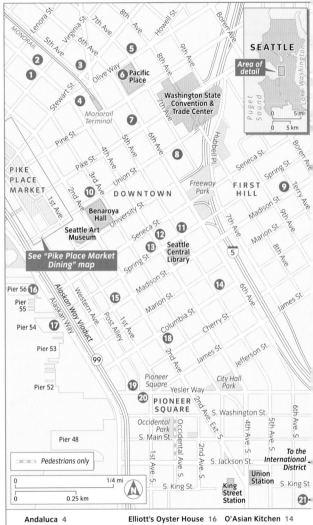

Andaluca 4
Assaggio 2
BOKA Kitchen + Bar 15
Café Paloma 20
China Gate 21
Coldwater Bar and Grill 3
Dahlia Lounge 1
Earth & Ocean 12

Elliott's Oyster House 16
Hunt Club 9
Il Fornaio 6
Ivar's Acres of Clams 17
Metropolitan Grill 18
Mitchelli's 19
Morton's The
Steakhouse 7

O'Asian Kitchen 14
The Oceanaire
Seafood Room 5
Sazerac 13
Tulio Ristorante 11
Union Square Grill 8
Wild Ginger 10

Pike Place Market Dining

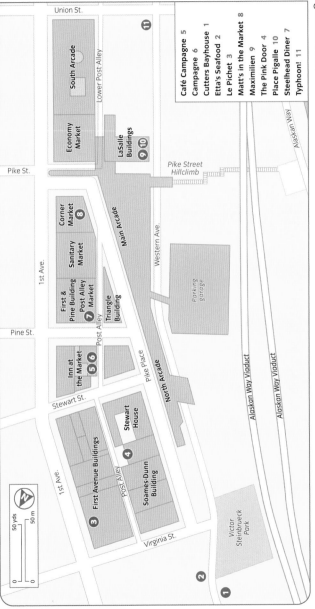

Café Campagne 5
Campagne 6
Cutters Bayhouse 1
Etta's Seafood 2
Le Pichet 3
Matt's in the Market 8
Maximilien 9
The Pink Door 4
Place Pigalle 10
Steelhead Diner 7
Typhoon! 11

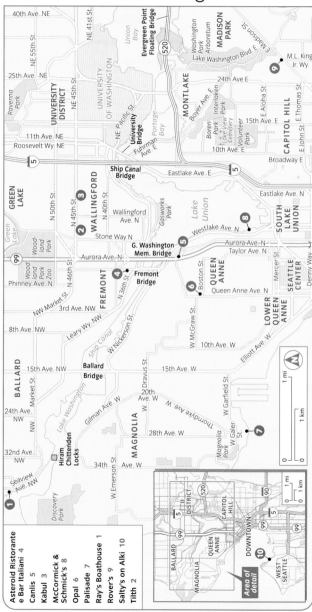

40th Ave. NE

NE 41st St.

NE 55th St.

NE 45th St.

25th Ave. NE

Evergreen Point Floating Bridge

520

Union Bay

Washington Park Arboretum

MADISON PARK

E Madison St.

M.L. King Jr. Wy.

❾

Ravenna Park

UNIVERSITY DISTRICT

NE 45th St.

UNIVERSITY OF WASHINGTON

24th Ave E

MONTLAKE

Boyer Ave. E

Interlaken Park

E Aloha St.

15th Ave. E

E Thomas St.

CAPITOL HILL

NE Pacific St.

Portage Bay

Boren Park

Lake View Cemetery

Volunteer Park

10th Ave. E

E John St.

11th Ave. NE

University Bridge

Fuhrman Ave. E

Broadway E

Roosevelt Wy. NE

5

Ship Canal Bridge

Eastlake Ave. E

5

Eastlake Ave. N

GREEN LAKE

N 50th St.

N 45th St.

❸

WALLINGFORD

N 40th St.

Wallingford Ave. N

Gasworks Park

Lake Union

Westlake Ave. N

❽

SOUTH LAKE UNION

Green Lake

Wood-land Park

❷

Stone Way N

Aurora Ave. N

99

Woodland Park Zoo

Phinney Ave. N

N 46th St.

❹

FREMONT

Fremont Bridge

N 36th St.

G. Washington Mem. Bridge

❺

Aurora Ave. N

Taylor Ave. N

Boston St.

❻

QUEEN ANNE

Queen Anne Ave. N

Mercer St.

SEATTLE CENTER

Denny Way

NW Market St.

3rd Ave. NW

Leary Wy. NW

N Nickerson St.

Ship Canal

W McGraw St.

LOWER QUEEN ANNE

8th Ave. NW

10th Ave. W

Elliott Ave. W

BALLARD

15th Ave. NW

Market St.

Ballard Bridge

15th Ave. W

Dravus St.

W Garfield St.

N

1 mi

1 km

24th Ave. NW

Gilman Ave. W

20th Ave. W

28th Ave. W

Thorndyke Ave. W

MAGNOLIA

W Galer St.

❼

Magnolia Park

32nd Ave. NW

Hiram Chittenden Locks

34th Ave. W

0   1 mi

0   1 km

Seaview Ave. NW

❶

Discovery Park

W Emerson St.

U DISTRICT

520

90

5

CAPITOL HILL

5

BALLARD

99

99

99

MAGNOLIA

QUEEN ANNE

DOWNTOWN

❿

WEST SEATTLE

Area of detail

0   1 mi

0   1 km

Asteroid Ristorante e Bar Italiani	4
Canlis	5
Kabul	3
McCormick's & Schmick's	8
Opal	6
Palisade	7
Ray's Boathouse	1
Rover's	9
Salty's on Alki	10
Tilth	2

Restaurants **A to Z**

★★ **Andaluca** DOWNTOWN
MEDITERRANEAN Spain meets
the Northwest in perfectly spiced
paellas and other Mediterranean-
influenced choices. The romantic
Andaluca is at the Mayflower Park
Hotel. *407 Olive Way.* ☎ *206/382-
6999. Entrees $23–$52. AE, DC, MC,
V. Breakfast & dinner daily, lunch
Mon–Fri. Monorail or bus: 10, 11,
12, 49. Map p 112.*

★★ **Assaggio** DOWNTOWN
ITALIAN From the Michelangelo-
inspired art to the personal welcome
by gregarious owner/chef Mauro
Golmarvi to the melt-in-your-mouth
veal dishes, there's no doubt you've
entered a world where food is a pas-
sion. The boisterous back room is a
fun place to meet friends; the front
room has more private spaces. Leave
room for dessert. *2010 4th Ave.*
☎ *206/441-1399. Entrees $13–$28.
AE, DC, DISC, MC, V. Lunch Mon–Fri,
dinner Mon–Sat. Bus: 70. Map p 112.*

★ **Asteroid Ristorante e Bar
Italiani** NORTH SEATTLE *ITALIAN*
At this popular neighborhood bistro
in Fremont, a wide array of fresh
pastas and entrees are served in a
casually elegant space. *3601 Fremont
Ave. N.* ☎ *206/547-9000. Entrees
$14–$26. AE, DC, DISC, MC, V. Dinner
daily. Bus: 5, 26, 28. Map p 114.*

★★ **BOKA Kitchen + Bar**
DOWNTOWN *NEW AMERICAN*
Food is art, and art is food for the
soul at this stylish cafe in the ultrahip Hotel 1000. It's hard to decide
whether to take a bite or a picture—
but my advice is, take a bite! The flavorful, inventive menu shifts with
the season. The petrale sole is fabulous. *1000 1st Ave.* ☎ *206/357-9000.
Entrees $21–$30. MC, V. Lunch
Mon–Fri, brunch Sat–Sun, dinner
daily. Bus: 10, 12, 16. Map p 112.*

★★ **Brasa** BELLTOWN *MEDITER-
RANEAN* This lovely eatery adds a
dash of creativity to even the most
basic dish. Try the juicy roast pork,
and you'll see what I mean. The
lounge has a less pricey—but very
good—menu. *2107 3rd Ave.* ☎ *206/
728-4220. Entrees $24–$32. AE, DC,
DISC, MC, V. Dinner daily. Bus: 1, 2,
3, 4, 16. Map p 111.*

★★ **Café Campagne** PIKE PLACE
MARKET *FRENCH* Sister restaurant
to the upscale Campagne (see

The art on the walls is as inventive as the cuisine at Assaggio.

below), the Café Campagne offers a casual, oh-so-French bistro experience. You won't find a better croquemonsieur outside Paris. *1600 Post Alley.* ☎ *206/728-2233. Entrees $17–$23. AE, DC, MC, V. Lunch Mon–Fri, brunch Sat–Sun, dinner daily. Bus: 11, 12, 15, 18, 21, 22, 49, 56. Map p 113.*

Café Paloma PIONEER SQUARE *MEDITERRANEAN* At this intimate Turkish cafe, you'll find Mediterranean standards, plus some creative choices—think gorgonzola panini. *93 Yesler Way.* ☎ *206/405-1920. Entrees $6–$10. MC, V. Lunch Mon–Sat, dinner Thurs–Sat. Bus: 15, 18, 21, 22, 56. Map p 112.*

★★★ Campagne PIKE PLACE MARKET *FRENCH* This is classic French country cooking—sunny southern France, to be precise—at its flavorful best. The seafood and game meats are fresh and local, as is the produce. From foie gras to steak frites to roast duck, the presentations are beautiful and the sauces outstanding. A prix-fixe menu is available, and in the summertime you can dine in a charming courtyard. *86 Pine St.* ☎ *206/728-*

The wine list is seemingly endless at Campagne.

2800. Entrees $25–$39. AE, DC, MC, V. Dinner daily. Bus: 11, 12, 15, 18, 21, 22, 49, 56. Map p 113.

★★★ Canlis DOWNTOWN *NORTH-WEST* Dining here is more an experience than a meal. The food is fabulous—fresh and inventive—and the wine list outstanding. The mango, prawn, and avocado salad is delightful; the lamb chops with couscous exquisite. But it's the service, impeccable without being stuffy, that makes Canlis perfect for a special occasion. Plan to spend longer than usual for dinner, because you won't want the pampering—or the view of Lake Union—to end. *2576 Aurora Ave N.* ☎ *206/283-3313. Entrees $28–$70. AE, DISC, MC, V. Dinner Mon–Sat. Bus: 15, 18, 21, 22, 56. Map p 114.*

★ kids China Gate INTERNATIONAL DISTRICT *CHINESE* My favorite thing here is the dim sum; you'll find one of the best selections in town at this casual spot. *516 7th Ave. S.* ☎ *206/624-1730. Entrees $6–$17. AE, MC, V. Lunch & dinner daily. Map p 112.*

★★ Coldwater Bar and Grill DOWNTOWN *SEAFOOD/NORTHWEST* This contemporary bistro in the Westin Seattle serves up fresh Northwest seafood, prepared with panache. The crab cakes are among the standouts on an imaginative regional menu. The raw bar offers a tasty sample of succulent Pacific Northwest oysters. *1900 5th Ave.* ☎ *206/256-7697. Entrees $21–$40. AE, MC, V. Breakfast, lunch & dinner daily. Bus: 70. Map p 112.*

★★ kids Cutters Bayhouse PIKE PLACE MARKET *NORTHWEST* This lovely restaurant is just steps from Pike Place Market. With sweeping views of Elliott Bay and friendly service, it's the perfect place to relax after shopping—and you won't feel uncomfortable bringing the kids (there's a children's menu). The seafood shines; try the tasty crab cakes. *2001 Western Ave.* ☎ *206/448-4884. Entrees $9.50–$40. AE, DC, DISC, MC, V. Breakfast Sat–Sun, lunch Mon–Sat, dinner daily. Bus: 11, 12, 15, 18, 21, 22, 49, 56. Map p 113.*

★★★ **Dahlia Lounge** BELLTOWN *NORTHWEST* The menu at this quintessential Seattle restaurant never fails to enchant with unique flavor combinations. Think five-spice Peking duck with curry fried rice and orange chili dip. Beautiful and elegant, Dahlia is owned by legendary chef Tom Douglas, who now runs six Seattle establishments, including a bakery. Leave room for dessert. *2001 4th Ave.* ☎ *206/682-4142. Entrees $22–$38. AE, DC, DISC, MC, V. Lunch & dinner daily. Bus: 70. Map p 112.*

kids Dick's Drive-In CAPITOL HILL *BURGERS* Seattle's iconic burger joint still has its original orange awnings from the '50s, though the drive-up service has ended. Many locals won't eat burgers anywhere else. *115 Broadway Ave. E.* ☎ *206/323-1300. Entrees $1.15–$2.20. Lunch & dinner daily. Bus: 49. Map p 111.*

★★ **Earth & Ocean** DOWNTOWN *NEW AMERICAN* Showcasing the best of the region from land and sea, this hip restaurant in the stylish W Hotel cures its own meats and offers a great chef's tasting menu, including an outstanding vegetarian option. At lunchtime, don't miss the truffle fries. *1112 4th Ave.* ☎ *206/264-6060. Entrees $28–$34. AE, DC, DISC, MC, V. Breakfast, lunch & dinner daily, brunch Sat–Sun. Bus: 2. Map p 112.*

★★ **El Gaucho** BELLTOWN *STEAK* The steaks are perfection, the service attentive at this upscale, supper-club-style steakhouse. For a truly special meal, order the chateaubriand for

Be sure to leave room for the desserts at Canlis.

two. *2505 1st Ave.* ☎ *206/728-1337. Entrees $16–$125. AE, DC, MC, V. Dinner daily. Bus: 15, 18, 21, 22, 56. Map p 111.*

★★ **kids Elliott's Oyster House** WATERFRONT *SEAFOOD* This is an oyster-lover's nirvana, with a huge selection of local oysters, served raw, steamed, or pan-fried. All the seafood here is fresh and local, with standouts including the salmon (always non-farmed) and the Dungeness crab with chili-lime sauce. If it's a nice day, dine outside on the deck overhanging Elliott Bay. *1201 Alaskan Way, Pier 56.* ☎ *206/623-4340. Entrees $18–$38. AE, DC, DISC, MC, V. Lunch & dinner daily. Bus: 99. Map p 112.*

★★ **Etta's Seafood** PIKE PLACE MARKET *SEAFOOD* Casual but tasteful, Etta's caters to the tourist crowd (you can even get a burger) but also has a loyal local following. Owned by chef Tom Douglas, Etta's is my favorite destination for salmon (you can buy the rub to take home). Another sure bet is Tom's famous Dungeness crab cakes. *2020 Western Ave.* ☎ *206/443-6000. Entrees $12–$33. AE, DC, DISC, MC, V. Lunch Mon–Fri, brunch Sat–Sun, dinner daily. Bus: 11, 12, 15, 18, 21, 22, 49, 56. Map p 113.*

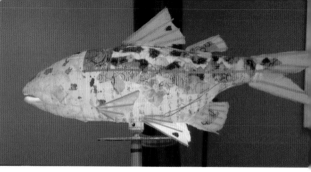

The decor is nearly as big a draw as the food at Dahlia Lounge (p 117).

Galerias CAPITOL HILL *MEXICAN*
This is a lovely spot to linger in. I'm partial to the vegetarian tamales, made of spinach corn dough and stuffed with feta and poblano chilis. *611 Broadway E.* ☎ *206/322-5757. Entrees $15–$18. AE, MC, V. Lunch & dinner daily. Bus: 49. Map p 111.*

★★★ Hunt Club FIRST HILL *NORTHWEST/MEDITERRANEAN*
Inside the elegant Sorrento Hotel, this warm, sophisticated restaurant elevates hotel dining to a new level. The Hunt Club delivers classic cuisine with imaginative touches, especially in its sauces. The duck with huckleberry sauce is a standout, and the black truffle mashed potatoes are not to be missed. Even worse would be missing the croissant bread pudding for dessert. *900 Madison St.* ☎ *206/343-6156. Entrees $15–$38. AE, DC, DISC, MC, V. Breakfast, lunch & dinner daily, brunch Sat–Sun. Bus: 12. Map p 112.*

★★ Il Fornaio DOWNTOWN *ITALIAN* With a new region of Italy featured each month, this stylish eatery delivers a new experience every time you come. The breads, baked on site, are divine; the sauces are scrumptious; and many of the wines come from Il Fornaio's own vineyard in Tuscany. My favorite dish: the ravioli stuffed with butternut squash and walnuts. The bakery and cafe are downstairs; climb the spiral staircase to the chic dining room. *600 Pine St., Ste. 132.* ☎ *206/264-0994. Entrees $12–$33. AE, DC, MC, V. Breakfast, lunch & dinner daily. Bus: 70. Map p 112.*

★ kids Ivar's Acres of Clams WATERFRONT *SEAFOOD* This iconic Seattle establishment, perched on Pier 54, has been in business in various forms for 70 years. It's a charming place to eat fresh seafood and watch the ferries cross the Sound. *1001 Alaskan Way.* ☎ *206/624-6852. Entrees $17–$40. AE, DISC, MC, V. Lunch Mon–Sat, brunch Sun, dinner daily. Bus: 99. Map p 112.*

★ Kabul NORTH SEATTLE *AFGHAN* I am not the biggest fan of eggplant, but Kabul transforms that humble vegetable into a dish so flavorful, it's my favorite entrée here. Finish the night with a cup of cardamom tea. *2301 N. 45th St.* ☎ *206/545-9000. Entrees $15–$21. AE, DC, DISC, MC, V. Dinner daily. Map p 114.*

★★ Lampreia BELLTOWN *ITALIAN/ NORTHWEST* The artful dishes here taste as wonderful as they look, which is saying a lot. *2400 1st. Ave.* ☎ *206/443-3301. Entrees $30–$45. AE, DISC, MC, V. Dinner daily. Bus: 15, 18, 21, 22, 56. Map p 111.*

★★ Lark CAPITOL HILL *INTERNATIONAL* This trendy bistro has earned a name for service and quality. The eclectic menu ranges from scrambled eggs with truffles to caviar with potatoes and cream. *926 12th Ave.* ☎ *206/323-5275. Entrees $11–$20. MC, V. Dinner Tues–Sun. Bus: 2, 10. Map p 111.*

★★ **Le Pichet** PIKE PLACE MARKET *FRENCH* This casual bistro serves a classic French menu that would make a Parisian feel right at home. The ingredients are simple and fresh; the sauces superb. The roast chicken takes an hour to make once you've ordered it, but it's worth every minute. *1933 1st Ave.* ☎ *206/ 256-1499. Entrees $18–$19. MC, V. Casse-croute (pastry/snacks) daily, lunch & dinner daily. Bus: 11, 12, 15, 18, 21, 22, 49, 56. Map p 113.*

★★ **Marazul** SOUTH LAKE UNION *CARIBBEAN/ASIAN* At this beautiful space adjacent to the Pan Pacific Hotel, the dishes are delightfully out of the ordinary. For lunch, my favorite is the Caribbean bento box, with its fabulous Jamaican-style curried chicken, shrimp seviche, and plantains. Vegetarians will love the flavorful Asian bento box. Sauces are made with coconut milk; sushi and tapas are available. *2200 Westlake Ave.* ☎ *206/654-8170. Entrees $11–$17. AE, MC, V. Breakfast, lunch & dinner daily. South Lake Union Streetcar to 9th Ave.*

★ **Marco's Supperclub** BELLTOWN *INTERNATIONAL* Diners can travel the world without leaving Belltown at this charming spot—always expect the unexpected on the menu. Don't miss the light, crispy fried sage leaves with dipping sauces. *2510 1st Ave.* ☎ *206/441-7801. Entrees $17–$24. AE, MC, V. Dinner daily. Bus: 15, 18, 21, 22, 56. Map p 111.*

★ **Marrakesh Moroccan Restaurant** BELLTOWN *MOROCCAN* This cozy place has the feel of an Arabian tent. Diners sit on cushions or benches at round tables as

tantalizing aromas and belly dancers (Fri and Sat) drift through the room. *2334 2nd Ave.* ☎ *206/956-0500. Entrees $17–$19. DISC, MC, V. Dinner Tues–Sun. Bus: 15, 18, 21, 22, 56. Map p 111.*

★★ **Matt's in the Market** PIKE PLACE MARKET *NORTHWEST* Chef Chester Gerl doesn't have far to go to get market-fresh produce and seafood. Matt's expanded location is right above Pike Place Market. *94 Pike St., Ste. 32.* ☎ *206/467-7909. MC, V. Entrees $22–$33. Lunch Mon–Sat, dinner Tues–Sat. Bus: 11, 12, 15, 18, 21, 22, 49, 56. Map p 113.*

★★ **Maximilien in the Market** PIKE PLACE MARKET. *FRENCH* Watch the sun set over Elliott Bay through panoramic windows as you dine on classic French fare. *81A Pike St.* ☎ *206/682-7270. AE, DC, DISC, MC, V. Entrees $20–$45. Lunch & dinner daily, brunch Sat–Sun. Bus: 11, 12, 15, 18, 21, 22, 49, 56. Map p 113.*

★★ **McCormick & Schmick's** LAKE UNION *SEAFOOD* With a spectacular view of Lake Union and an outside deck, this elegant restaurant is a great spot for dinner. But it's also popular at lunchtime, when you can watch the seaplanes take off.

Metropolitan Grill (p 120).

Moxie is the perfect dinner spot if you're seeing a show at McCaw Hall.

Seafood is the star, and the "fresh list" is impressively long. Don't miss the bay shrimp cake appetizers. *1200 Westlake Ave. N.* ☎ *206/270-9052. Entrees $16–$40. AE, DC, DISC, MC, V. Lunch Mon–Fri, brunch Sat–Sun, dinner daily. Map p 114.*

★★★ **Metropolitan Grill** DOWN-TOWN *STEAKS* This historic Seattle restaurant could make a beef-eater out of anyone. If you're in the mood for extravagance, order the prized wagyu steak. But the steak on the regular menu is so flavorful, and cooked to such perfection, there's no need to look further. At lunchtime, it's very popular with the business crowd. *820 2nd Ave.* ☎ *206/624-3287. Entrees $22–$140. AE, DC, DISC, MC, V. Lunch Mon–Fri, dinner daily. Bus: 16, 358. Map p 112.*

kids **Mitchelli's** PIONEER SQUARE *ITALIAN* Come here for a late-night dinner after an evening out in Pioneer Square. It's open till 4am Fridays and Saturdays. The menu includes wood-fired pizzas, pasta, and salads. *84 Yesler Way.* ☎ *206/ 682-4757. Lunch Mon–Fri, brunch Sat–Sun, dinner daily. Entrees $10– $14. AE, DISC, MC, V. Bus: 16, 99. Map p 112.*

★★ **Morton's The Steakhouse** DOWNTOWN *STEAKS* This classic steakhouse is reminiscent of a glamorous era of crisp, white linens; rich cherry wood; and tuxedoed waiters. The service is excellent without being obtrusive; the steaks divine. My favorite? The melt-in-your-mouth filet mignon. The lengthy wine list includes an unusually interesting by-the-glass selection. *1511 6th Ave.* ☎ *206/223-0550. Entrees $31–$102. AE, DC, DISC, MC, V. Dinner daily. Bus: 10, 12. Map p 112.*

★★ **Moxie** QUEEN ANNE *SEAFOOD/AMERICAN* At this beautiful bistro, a favorite spot for event-goers at McCaw Hall and the Seattle Center, Chef Lauri Carter indeed puts a lot of moxie into her menu, infusing it with creative flavor combinations. Seafood dishes excel, but the *osso buco* also melts in the mouth, and the boldly flavored chile relleno is simultaneously rich and light as air. Be sure to try the sweet potato fries. *530 1st Ave. N.* ☎ *206/ 283-6614. Entrees $18–$30. AE, MC, V. Dinner daily. Bus: 1, 2, 13, 15, 18. Map p 111.*

★ **O'Asian Kitchen** DOWNTOWN *CHINESE* This stylish restaurant is a relative newcomer. The best thing is the dim sum, popular with the office lunch crowd, that comes steaming from the kitchen on traditional carts. *800 5th Ave.* ☎ *206/ 264-1789. Entrees $9–$26. AE, MC, V. Lunch, dinner & dim sum daily. Bus: 10. Map p 112.*

★★ **The Oceanaire Seafood Room** DOWNTOWN *SEAFOOD* Oceanaire offers an extensive menu of fresh, creatively prepared delights from the sea. The menu includes fish not often found on Seattle menus, such as Thai snapper. *1700 7th Ave.* ☎ *206/267-2277. Entrees $19–$100. AE, DC, DISC, MC, V. Lunch Mon–Fri, dinner daily. Bus: 11, 12, 49. Map p 112.*

★★ **Opal** QUEEN ANNE *NEW AMERI-CAN* This trendy new bistro tries daring flavor combinations, and comes up with some real winners. Think sweet potato French toast with foie gras. *2 Boston St.* ☎ *206/282-0142. Entrees $24–$29. AE, DISC, MC, V. Dinner Mon–Sat. Map p 114.*

★★ kids **Pagliacci Pizza** CAPITOL HILL *PIZZA* The pies here come with thin, crunchy crusts and bold, tasty toppings. Try a slice of pesto primo with garlic sauce, topped with fontina, mozzarella, and ricotta. *426 Broadway Ave. E.* ☎ *206/726-1717. Entrees $14–$23. MC, V. Lunch & dinner daily. Bus: 49. Map p 111.*

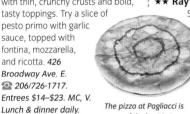

The pizza at Pagliacci is some of the best in town.

★★ **Palisade** NORTH SEATTLE *NORTHWEST/POLYNESIAN* This landmark Seattle restaurant has a Polynesian influence. The panoramic views of Elliott Bay, Mt. Rainier, and the city are stunning; the seafood fresh and expertly prepared. Start with the lemongrass calamari; finish with a clever bento box dessert, packed with goodies such as jasmine rice and mango tapioca "sushi." *2601 W. Marina Place.* ☎ *206/285-1000. Entrees $23–$54. AE, DC, DISC, MC, V. Lunch Mon–Fri, brunch Sun, dinner daily. Map p 114.*

★★ **The Pink Door** PIKE PLACE MARKET *ITALIAN* The best way to spot this funky, beloved cafe is to look for the pink door. If it's a sunny day, ask for a table on the spectacular deck. At night, you can hear lively music from the adjoining lounge. And if you care to stay late on Saturday, for another $12 you can watch the cabaret. The food is delicious; try the gnocchi with spinach. *1919 Post Alley.* ☎ *206/443-3241. Entrees $13–$24. AE, MC, V. Lunch & dinner Tues–Sun. Bus: 11, 12, 15, 18, 21, 22, 49, 56. Map p 113.*

★★ **Place Pigalle** PIKE PLACE MARKET *FRENCH* You can't beat

the mussels at this romantic spot perched above the Sound, where you'll dine to the strains of Edith Piaf. *81 Pike St.* ☎ *206/624-1756 Entrees $24–$37. AE, DC, DISC, MC, V. Lunch & dinner Mon–Sat. Bus: 11, 12, 15, 18, 21, 22, 49, 56. Map p 113.*

★★ **Ray's Boathouse** NORTH SEATTLE *SEAFOOD* An iconic seafood restaurant in the Ballard neighborhood, Ray's menu is as fresh and delicious as ever. The view, looking out over the Puget Sound, is jaw-dropping. Families with kids may opt for the more casual cafe. *6049 Seaview Ave. NW.* ☎ *206/789-3770. Entrees $24–$40. AE, DC, DISC, MC, V. Lunch & dinner Tues–Sun. Map p 114.*

Ray's Boathouse is a Seattle institution thanks to its superb seafood.

★★ **Rosebud** CAPITOL HILL *AMERICAN* This popular bistro, housed in a beautiful, romantic space, focuses on organic and free-range items. The welcome is warm, the dishes creative and delicious. The weekend brunch is very reasonable and includes unusual offerings, such as lavender lambchetta and andouille scramble. My advice: Try the stuffed French toast. *719 E. Pike St.* ☎ *206/323-6636. Entrees $15–$26. AE, DC, DISC, MC, V. Brunch Sat–Sun; dinner daily. Bus: 10, 11, 49. Map p 111.*

★★★ **Rover's** DOWNTOWN *FRENCH* Famed Chef Thierry Rautureau produces a new menu every day, with dishes built around fresh local ingredients and prepared with French élan. *2808 E. Madison St.* ☎ *206/325-7442. Entrees (tasting-size) $18–$23; 5-course tasting menu $95. AE, DC, MC, V. Lunch Fri, dinner Tues–Sat. Map p 114.*

★★ kids **Salty's on Alki** WEST SEATTLE *SEAFOOD* The panoramic view looking across the bay at Seattle is an eye-popper—but so is the brunch buffet, laden with fresh seafood, pasta, and omelets to order (try the lobster-filled pasta), meats, and more. The gingerbread pancakes are addictive! But save room for the dessert buffet, starring a chocolate fountain. Or come for a sunset dinner. *1936 Harbor Ave. SW.* ☎ *206/937-1600. Entrees $20–$32. AE, DC, DISC, MC, V. Lunch Mon–Fri, brunch Sat–Sun, dinner daily. Map p 114.*

★★ **Sazerac** DOWNTOWN *AMERICAN/SOUTHERN* The focus at this New Orleans-influenced restaurant in the beautiful Monaco Hotel is as much on fun as it is on food, and it gets them both right. You can't get better catfish this side of the Mississippi, period. And order whatever bread pudding is on the menu. *1101 4th Ave.* ☎ *206/624-7755. Entrees $13–$26. AE, DISC, MC, V. Breakfast, lunch & dinner daily. Bus: 2. Map p 112.*

★★ **Shiro's** BELLTOWN *SUSHI* Try to get a seat at the sushi bar, where you can watch legendary sushi Chef Shiro Kashiba work his genial magic. *2401 2nd Ave.* ☎ *206/443-9844. Entrees $2–$24. AE, DISC, MC, V. Dinner daily. Bus: 3, 4, 13, 16. Map p 111.*

★★ **Six Seven** WATERFRONT *SEAFOOD* Located in the historic Edgewater Hotel (where the Beatles once stayed), the Six Seven feels like a cozy lodge. It showcases the best of the region's seafood, accompanied by sides and appetizers that put local organic produce to

Six Seven offers the best of both worlds: excellent food and excellent views.

creative use. My favorite entrée is the sea bass, cooked to juicy perfection with a crispy skin. Holiday brunches are spectacular. The view of Elliott Bay is dramatic; in the summertime you can eat outside. *2411 Alaskan Way.* ☎ *206/269-4575. Entrees: $26–$48. AE, DC, DISC, MC, V. Breakfast & dinner daily, lunch Mon–Sat, brunch Sun. Bus: 99. Map p 111.*

★ **SkyCity at the Needle** DOWNTOWN *NORTHWEST* The menu features well-prepared local seafood, berries, and other produce, but the main attraction is the view. You'll see Seattle from every angle as you rotate around the Space Needle. Observation deck admission is included. *400 Broad St.* ☎ *206/905-2100. Entrees $34–$65. AE, DC, DISC, MC, V. Monorail or bus: 3, 4, 16. Map p 111.*

★★ **Steelhead Diner** PIKE PLACE MARKET *SEAFOOD/NEW AMERICAN* This lively new spot features the cooking of Kevin Davis, who brings together influences of New Orleans, France, California, and the Northwest, making for a unique and exciting dining experience. Don't miss the fried cheese curds with mustard vinaigrette, using cheese from the market; or the caviar pie, a creamy concoction topped with a variety of roe. Other standouts: Oregon petrale sole, and a fabulous veggie "meatloaf." *5 Pine St.* ☎ *206/625-0129. Entrees $16–$29. AE, DISC, MC, V. Lunch Tues–Fri, brunch Sat–Sun, dinner Mon–Sat. Bus: 11, 12, 15, 18, 21, 22, 49, 56. Map p 113.*

★★ **Tavolata** BELLTOWN *ITALIAN* This hip new urban space serves up mouthwatering Italian dishes, always with more than a dash of ingenuity. The menu changes daily, so you'll find linguine with mussels one day while the next it may come with chili and prosciutto. The mozzarella is homemade, as are the succulent pastas. The seafood is just as outstanding. *2323 2nd Ave.* ☎ *206/838-8008. Entrees $14–$48. AE, DISC, MC, V. Dinner daily. Bus: 16, 358. Map p 111.*

★★ **Tilth** NORTH SEATTLE *ORGANIC/ NEW AMERICAN* This cozy restaurant in a Craftsman house specializes in showcasing the organic bounty of the region. It is one of few establishments across the nation to have acquired official organic certification. *1411 N. 45th St.* ☎ *206/633-0801. Entrees $12–$29. MC, V. Dinner Tues–Sun, brunch Sat–Sun. Map p 114.*

★★ **Tulio Ristorante** DOWNTOWN *ITALIAN* The pasta is painstakingly handmade at this warm, inviting spot, a favorite among theatergoers. Chef Walter Pisano, who named the establishment for his restaurateur-father, is a maestro at Italian cooking with contemporary flair. One repeat customer comes from Canada just for the sweet potato gnocchi, and when you taste it you'll know why. *2323 2nd Ave., at the Hotel Vintage Park.* ☎ *206/ 838-8008. Entrees $14–$35. AE, DC, DISC, MC, V. Bus: 2. Map p 112.*

★★ **Txori** BELLTOWN *SPANISH/ TAPAS* This hot new restaurant serves real tapas—tiny portions of delicacies that arrive looking like works of art. The cocktails and coffee drinks are also delicious. *2207 2nd Ave.* ☎ *206/204-9771. Tapas $2–$6. MC, V. Lunch & dinner daily. Bus: 15, 18, 21, 22, 56. Map p 111.*

★★ **Typhoon!** PIKE PLACE MARKET *THAI* Noodles never tasted so good. Actually, noodles are just the beginning of the offerings at this chic restaurant, which serves Thai food with a contemporary twist. I usually go for the juicy, flavorful seafood dishes; if banana-leaf-wrapped trout is on the menu, don't

The Steelhead Diner (p 123) offers one of the most creative menus in Seattle.

pass it up. Vegetarian options are bursting with flavor, and vegan requests are happily met. *1400 Western Ave.* ☎ *206/262-9797. Entrees $9–$24. Lunch Mon–Sat, dinner daily. AE, DC, DISC, MC, V. Bus: 11, 12, 15, 18, 21, 22, 49, 56. Map p 113.*

★★ **Union Square Grill** DOWN-TOWN *NEW AMERICAN* Equally popular with the business lunch crowd and theatergoers, this elegant restaurant boasts an eclectic and inventive menu. The vegetable lasagna is bursting with flavor; the fish and meat dishes are lovingly prepared and accompanied by fresh local produce. *621 Union St.* ☎ *206/224-4321. Entrees $26–$32. AE,*

DISC, MC, V. Lunch Sun–Fri, dinner daily. Map p 112.

★★ **Veil** SOUTH LAKE UNION *NEW AMERICAN* Veils are the theme at this ultrahip spot: Gauzy curtains veil the windows; layers of food veil tasty layers below. Chef Shannon Galusha puts an extraordinary amount of thought into his menu: The Thai-spiced butternut squash soup is silky with crème fraîche and chili oil; the lake trout is perfect, with crispy skin and yummy cider puree. *555 Aloha St.* ☎ *206/216-0600. Entrees $11–$32. AE, MC, V. Dinner Tues–Sun, brunch Sat–Sun. Bus: 3, 4, 6. Map p 111.*

★★ **Wild Ginger** DOWNTOWN *PAN-ASIAN* This wildly popular restaurant is sophisticated, glamorous, and a boasts a very tempting menu. You can't go wrong with the Wild Ginger fragrant duck. There's a terrific separate vegetarian menu. *1401 3rd Ave.* ☎ *206/623-4450. Entrees $8–$30. AE, DC, DISC, MC. Lunch Mon–Sat, dinner daily. Bus: 1, 2, 3, 4, 13, 16. Map p 112.*

★★ kids **Zeek's** DOWNTOWN *PIZZA* The crust is to die for; the toppings are unconventional. Try the Tree-Hugger, with mozzarella, sun-dried tomato, spinach, mushroom, artichoke hearts, broccoli, tomato, garlic, and olives. *419 Denny Way.* ☎ *206/285-8646. Entrees $16–$22. MC, V. Lunch & dinner daily. Bus: 3, 4, 16. Map p 111.* ●

Nightlife Best Bets

Best Bartenders
★★ ZigZag Café, *1501 Western Ave.* (p 132)

Best Date Spot
★★ BOKA Kitchen + Bar, *1000 1st Ave.* (p 129)

Best Brewpub
★★ Elysian Brewing Company, *1221 E. Pike St* (p 130); and ★ The Pike Pub & Brewery, *1415 1st Ave.* (p 131)

Best Mariners Game-Day Hangout
★ Pyramid, *1201 1st Ave. S.* (p 132)

Best Sonics Game-Day Hangout
★ McMenamins, *300 Roy St., Ste. 105* (p 131)

Best Jazz Club
★★★ Dimitriou's Jazz Alley, *2033 6th Ave.* (p 133)

Best Happy Hour
★ Contour, *807 1st Ave.* (p 132); and Noc Noc, *1516 2nd Ave.* (p 133)

Best Hotel Bar
★★ Oliver's Lounge, *405 Olive Way* (p 131)

Best Bar Burger
Two Bells, *2313 4th Ave.* (p 132)

Best Bar to Run Into Your College Roommate
★★ Bookstore Bar, *1009 1st Ave.* (p 129)

Best Bar to Combine Spirits from Two Worlds
★★ Chapel, *1600 Melrose Ave.* (p 130)

Best Place to Drink Tequila
Del Rey, *2332 1st Ave.* (p 130)

Best Lesbian Bar
Wild Rose, *1021 E. Pike St.* (p 134)

Best Place to Dance in Pioneer Square
★ Last Supper Club, *124 S. Washington St.* (p 132)

Best Place to See and Be Seen
★★ Vessel, *1312 5th Ave.* (p 132)

Best Martinis
★ Karma Martini Lounge & Bistro, *2318 2nd Ave.* (p 130)

Best Gay-Friendly Bar
★ Neighbours, *1509 Broadway* (p 134)

Best Place to Dance with the Beautiful People
★★ Baltic Room, *1207 Pine St.* (p 132)

Try the cocktails at Chapel.

Pioneer Square Nightlife

88 Keys Dueling Piano Sports Bar 23

Alibi Room 6

BOKA Kitchen + Bar 11

Bookstore Bar 12

The Central Saloon 22

Contour 13

Doc Maynard's 16

Fado Irish Pub 14

J&M Café & Cardroom 21

Kells Irish Restaurant & Pub 3

Last Supper Club 20

Marcus' Martini Heaven 17

New Orleans 19

Noc Noc 4

Oliver's Lounge 1

Owl 'N Thistle 15

The Pike Pub & Brewery 7

Pyramid Alehouse 25

Slugger's 24

Tap House Grill 2

Trinity Night Club 18

The Triple Door 8

Vessel 9

W Bar 10

ZigZag Café 5

Downtown Nightlife

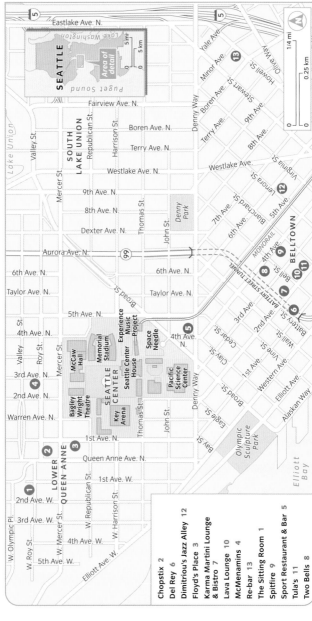

Chopstix 2
Del Rey 6
Dimitriou's Jazz Alley 12
Floyd's Place 3
Karma Martini Lounge & Bistro 7
Lava Lounge 10
McMenamins 4
Re-bar 13
The Sitting Room 1
Spitfire 9
Sport Restaurant & Bar 5
Tula's 11
Two Bells 8

Capitol Hill Nightlife

Baltic Room **2**	Elysian Brewing	Martins Off
Cha Cha Lounge **6**	Company **9**	Madison **11**
Chapel **3**	Fireside Room **1**	Neighbours **5**
Chop Suey **10**	Licorous **13**	Purr **7**
The Cuff	Linda's Tavern **4**	The Wild Rose **6**
Complex **8**	Madison Pub **12**	

Nightlife **A to Z**

Bars & Lounges

★ **Alibi Room** PIKE PLACE MAR-KET   Tucked away beneath the Market, this hip pub serves up potent drinks and very good food. Club nights with dance DJs are Fridays and Saturdays, in the downstairs room. *85 Pike St., Ste. 410.* ☎ *206/623-3180. Bus: 15, 18, 21, 22, 56. Map p 127.*

★★ **BOKA Kitchen + Bar** DOWN-TOWN   This contemporary bar is a beautiful place to relax and enjoy gourmet bar food—the pear and blue cheese bruschetta, perhaps, or the sugar-cane-skewered crab cakes. The seasonal cocktails are fun and delicious. *1000 1st Ave.* ☎ *206/357-9000. Bus: 10, 12, 16. Map p 127.*

★★ **Bookstore Bar** DOWNTOWN This elegant bar at the Alexis Hotel makes you feel like you're enjoying drinks in a well-heeled friend's private library. *1009 1st Ave.* ☎ *206/ 382-1506. Bus: 15, 18, 21, 22, 56. Map p 127.*

The Central Saloon PIONEER SQUARE   The oldest saloon in Seattle, the Central is a favorite neighborhood hangout. The food is good, and the live rock can be fabulous. *207 1st Ave. S.* ☎ *206/622-0209. Cover $5–$10 (or joint Pioneer Square cover $5 Sun–Thurs, $10 Fri–Sat). Bus: 15, 18, 21, 22, 56. Map p 127.*

Cha Cha Lounge CAPITOL HILL Red lighting, kitschy velvet paintings, piñatas hanging from the ceiling—

the Cha Cha Lounge has personality to spare. Punk and heavy metal shake the rafters. Get your nachos upstairs at Bimbo's Cantina. *1013 E. Pike St.* ☎ *206/322-0703. Bus: 10, 11, 49. Map p 129.*

★ **Chapel** CAPITOL HILL This stylish bar is housed in a former funeral home, but it's anything but morbid. Chapel makes good use of its building's history; even the bar is made from a mausoleum. *1600 Melrose Ave.* ☎ *206/447-4180. Bus: 10, 11, 49. Map p 129.*

Del Rey BELLTOWN A great place to see and be seen, this Art Deco lounge serves excellent food and an amazing variety of tequilas. And you get two happy hours—one from 4 to 7pm; one from 11pm to 1am. *2332 1st Ave.* ☎ *206/770-3228. Bus: 15, 18, 21, 22, 56. Map p 128.*

Doc Maynard's PIONEER SQUARE One of the most popular bars in Pioneer Square, Doc Maynard's is named for the Seattle co-founder—a bit of a drinker himself. Doc Maynard's features live local rock on Friday and Saturday nights. *610 1st Ave.* ☎ *206/682-3705. Cover $8. Bus: 16, 358. Map p 127.*

★★ **Elysian Brewing Company** CAPITOL HILL This award-winning microbrewery offers great beer and great food. A customer favorite is the Avatar Jasmine, an India pale ale

The Central Saloon (p 129) is a Seattle institution.

brewed with jasmine flowers. *1221 E. Pike St.* ☎ *206/860-1920. Bus: 12. Map p 129.*

★ **Fado Irish Pub** PIONEER SQUARE Throw back a pint of Irish ale with the regulars at this popular after-work tavern. They also serve up a mean corned beef and cabbage. Irish bands play frequently. *801 1st Ave.* ☎ *206/264-2700. $5 cover after 9pm Fri–Sat. Bus: 15, 18, 21, 22, 56. Map p 127.*

★★ **Fireside Room** FIRST HILL This elegant lounge at the Sorrento Hotel is a romantic spot for a drink, especially on Friday and Saturday nights, when you can hear live music, usually jazz. *900 Madison St.* ☎ *206/343-6156. Bus: 12. Map p 129.*

J&M Café & Cardroom PIONEER SQUARE This beautiful old saloon still draws the crowds, which grow younger—and less inhibited—when it's time for dancing. Local bands play Sun–Thurs. *201 1st Ave. S.* ☎ *206/292-0663. Cover none–$10 (or joint Pioneer Square cover $5 Sun–Thurs, $10 Fri–Sat). Bus: 15, 18, 21, 22, 56. Map p 127.*

★ **Karma Martini Lounge & Bistro** BELLTOWN You've never had martinis like they make them at Karma. Think cucumber. Think Washington apple. Think delicious. *2318 2nd Ave.* ☎ *206/838-6018. Bus: 26, 28. Map p 128.*

★ **Kells Irish Restaurant & Pub** PIKE PLACE MARKET If it's a nice day, settle in on the patio with a shepherd's pie and a pint, and enjoy the lively mixed crowd of tourists and students. There's generally live Irish music in the evenings. *1916 Post Alley.* ☎ *206/728-1916. $5 cover after 9pm Fri–Sat; higher for some bands. Bus: 15, 18, 21, 22, 56. Map p 127.*

Lava Lounge BELLTOWN Shuffleboard, pinball, and kitsch are the main attractions at this Tiki bar. No food is served—just nuts and chips—but there are DJs every night spinning hip-hop, funk, and heavy metal. *2226 2nd Ave.* ☎ *206/441-5660. Bus: 26, 28. Map p 128.*

Licorous CAPITOL HILL This elegant tavern mixes up yummy specialty cocktails, and has a terrific menu prepared by the wonderful chef at sister restaurant Lark. *928 12th Ave.* ☎ *206/325-6947. Map p 129.*

Linda's Tavern CAPITOL HILL Order a pitcher of beer and settle back to people-watch at this eclectic neighborhood bar. You're as likely to see punk rockers and country music fans. Linda's has a great menu with veggie options. *707 E. Pine St.* ☎ *206/325-1220. Bus: 10, 11, 49. Map p 129.*

★ **Marcus' Martini Heaven** PIO-NEER SQUARE Literally an underground hangout for tourists and hip urbanites, Marcus' boasts an amazing selection of martinis, as well as other drinks and food. DJs spin the tunes nightly. *88 Yesler Way.* ☎ *206/624-3323. Bus: 15, 18, 21, 22, 56. Map p 127.*

★ **McMenamins** QUEEN ANNE A popular pre-basketball game brewpub, McMenamins produces a fine selection of ales. The stick-to-your-ribs menu is also pleasing. *300*

Lave Lounge takes Tiki chic to a new level.

Roy St., Ste. 105. ☎ *206/285-4722. Bus: 1, 2, 13. Map p 128.*

★★ **Oliver's Lounge** DOWNTOWN This relaxing bar at the elegant Mayflower Park Hotel serves award-winning martinis and upscale bar food. *405 Olive Way.* ☎ *206/382-6995. Bus: 70. Map p 127.*

★ **Owl 'N Thistle** DOWNTOWN A popular Irish bar, the Owl 'N Thistle offers an eclectic variety of bands, including its own house Irish folk band, and a dance area. *808 Post Ave.* ☎ *206/621-7777. Cover none–$5, depending on band. Map p 127.*

★ **The Pike Pub & Brewery** PIKE PLACE MARKET One of the 10

Kells is one of Seattle best Irish pubs and the perfect place for a pint.

largest breweries in the state, Pike keeps customers coming back for labels like the Scotch Style Pike Kilt Lifter and Naughty Nellie. *1415 1st Ave.* ☎ *206/622-6044. Bus: 15, 18, 21, 22, 56. Map p 127.*

★ **Pyramid Alehouse** PIONEER SQUARE   There are two big draws here: the location (across the street from Safeco Field) and the beer (including the award-winning Pyramid Hefe Weizen and Apricot Weizen). On Mariners game days, it fills up fast. *1201 1st Ave. S.* ☎ *206/682-3377. Bus: 15, 18, 21, 22, 56. Map p 127.*

★★ **The Sitting Room** QUEEN ANNE   A cozy spot with more than a dash of Euro-style, The Sitting Room serves tasty specialty cocktails and gourmet eats at intimate candlelit tables. *108 W. Roy.* ☎ *206/285-2830. Bus: 15, 18. Map p 128.*

★ **Tap House Grill** DOWNTOWN   With more than 150 beers on tap and an excellent menu (including steaks and sushi), this upscale spot is a fun place to watch a game. *1506 6th Ave.* ☎ *206/816-3314. Bus: 10. Map p 127.*

Two Bells DOWNTOWN   A favorite neighborhood hangout, Two Bells serves beer, wine, and some of the best burgers in Seattle. *2313 4th Ave.* ☎ *206/441-3050. Bus: 26, 28. Map p 128.*

★★ **Vessel** DOWNTOWN   This ultrahip bar's atmosphere is more L.A. than Seattle, but the coolness is just in the decor—not in the attitude. *1312 5th Ave.* ☎ *206/652-5222. Bus: 10. Map p 127.*

★ **W Bar** DOWNTOWN   With elegant decor, a great happy hour, and gourmet bar food, the W is a favorite after-work gathering spot. *1112 4th Ave.* ☎ *206/264-6000. Bus: 2. Map p 127.*

★★ **ZigZag Café** PIKE PLACE MARKET   The bartenders at this upscale but friendly spot are practically magicians, and more than happy to fill you in on all their amazing cocktails, many made with fresh-squeezed juices. *1501 Western Ave.* ☎ *206/625-1146. Map p 127.*

Dance Clubs

★★ **Baltic Room** CAPITOL HILL   This chic, romantic club plays themed music from around the globe, some via DJs; some via live instrumentals. A fun clientele of varying ethnicities and sexual persuasions pack the small dance floor. *1207 Pine St.* ☎ *206/625-4444. www.thebalticroom.net. Cover none–$10. Bus: 10, 11, 49. Map p 129.*

Chop Suey CAPITOL HILL   The dance floor is usually packed at this eclectic bar. Bands and DJs range from punk to techno. *1325 E. Madison.* ☎ *206/324-8000. www.chopsuey.com. Cover none–$30. Bus: 10. Map p 129.*

★ **Contour** DOWNTOWN   This is where serious partiers dance till dawn to DJs and live bands. Happy hour on Friday lasts 5 hours, ending at 8pm, and a drink and appetizer costs $5. *807 1st Ave.* ☎ *206/447-7704. www.clubcontour.com. Cover none–$5. Bus: 15, 18, 21, 22, 56. Map p 127.*

★ **Last Supper Club** PIONEER SQUARE   This fashionable club spreads out over three floors, including a laser-lit dance floor. DJs keep a dressy crowd hopping. *124 S. Washington St.* ☎ *206/748-9975. www.lastsupperclub.com Cover none–$10 (or joint Pioneer Square cover $5*

Fans of jazz should plan to spend an evening at Dimitriou's Jazz Alley.

Sun–Thurs, $10 Fri–Sat). Bus: 99. Map p 127.

Noc Noc DOWNTOWN Known for its happy hour ($1 beer and the world's best $2 Tater Tots!) from 5–9pm weekdays, this friendly club packs 'em in. *1516 2nd Ave. ☎ 206/223-1333. www.clubnocnoc.com. Cover none–$10 (or joint Pioneer Square cover $5 Sun–Thurs, $10 Fri–Sat). Bus: 10. Map p 127.*

★ **Trinity Night Club** PIONEER SQUARE A young clientele dances its way through three floors, each with a different type of music, at this multi-level dance club. Come Tues–Fri for the unusual dim sum happy hour. *111 Yesler Way. ☎ 206/447-4140. Cover none–$15. Map p 127.*

Disco balls light up the room at Trinity.

Piano Bars

★ **Chopstix** QUEEN ANNE The fun starts at 8pm, when dueling musician/entertainers play their hearts out on a pair of grand pianos. *11 Roy St. ☎ 206/270-4444. Cover Fri & Sat $7. Bus: 1, 2, 13, 15, 18. Map p 128.*

★ **88 Keys Dueling Piano Sports Bar** PIONEER SQUARE An unlikely combination of dueling pianists and sports makes this a unique and entertaining spot. The show starts at 9pm. *315 2nd Ave. ☎ 206/839-1300. Cover $2–$5. Bus: 99. Map p 127.*

Live Jazz & Blues

★★★ **Dimitriou's Jazz Alley** BELLTOWN With consistently great acts from around the globe, this beautiful club is Seattle's premier jazz spot. *2033 6th Ave. ☎ 206/441-9729. Ticket prices vary; check website (www.jazzalley.com). Bus: 70. Map p 128.*

★ **Martins Off Madison** CAPITOL HILL A jazz bar with a grand piano and singers belting out the classics, Martins is a relaxing place to enjoy a drink and first-rate bar food. *1413 14th Ave. ☎ 206/325-7000. Bus: 2. Map p 129.*

★ **New Orleans** PIONEER SQUARE The New Orleans is hopping every night with live jazz, zydeco, and blues. Chow down on some Cajun food while you listen. *114 1st Ave. S. ☎ 206/622-2563. www.neworleanscreolerestaurant.com. Cover $8 Fri–Sat (or joint Pioneer Square cover $5 Sun–Thurs, $10 Fri–Sat). Bus: 15, 18, 21, 22, 56. Map p 127.*

★★ **The Triple Door** DOWNTOWN This former vaudeville theater attracts an upscale, friendly crowd. Hear music from around the world upstairs in the Musiquarium (a bar with a huge fish tank) or buy a ticket to watch the show in the Mainstage Theatre. Shows that start before 9pm are open to children. *216 Union St. ☎ 206/838-4343. www.tripledoor.com. Ticket prices vary; check website. Bus: 1, 2, 3, 4, 13, 16. Map p 127.*

★ **Tula's** BELLTOWN You'll find live jazz any night of the week at this intimate club, and a taste-tempting Mediterranean/American menu. It's an all-age venue until 10pm. *2214 2nd Ave. ☎ 206/443-4221. www.tulas.com. Cover $5–$20. Bus: 15, 18, 21, 22, 56. Map p 128.*

The Best Nightlife

Sports Bars

Floyd's Place QUEEN ANNE
Savor some of the best barbecue in town while you watch a game on one of many TV sets at this neighborhood hangout. Be prepared: It can get very crowded on a Sonics game day. *521 1st Ave. N.* ☎ *206/284-3542. Bus: 1, 2, 13. Map p 128.*

★ **Slugger's** PIONEER SQUARE
Across from Qwest Field and near Safeco Field, this convenient location draws lots of pre- and post-game fans. The walls are lined with Seattle sports memorabilia. *567 Occidental Ave. S.* ☎ *206/654-8070. Bus: 15, 18, 21, 22, 56. Map p 127.*

★ **Spitfire** BELLTOWN   Lots and lots of TV sets airing lots and lots of sports. Grab a bowl of yummy tortilla soup, loaded with avocado, or a pulled pork sandwich, and settle in. *2219 4th Ave.* ☎ *206/441-7966. Bus: 26, 28. Map p 128.*

★ **Sport Restaurant & Bar**
QUEEN ANNE   If you get a booth,

Spitfire is proof that even sports bars can be funky when they're done right.

you can control your own TV set. If not, don't worry, you'll have plenty of options, including the gargantuan HD screen over the lounge. *140 4th Ave. N., Ste. 130.* ☎ *206/404-7767. Bus: 3, 4, 16. Map p 128.*

Gay & Lesbian Bars & Clubs

The Cuff Complex CAPITOL HILL
This very popular gay bar draws mostly men. It has pool tables, pinball, a small dance floor, and nice outdoor deck in the back. *1533 13th Ave.* ☎ *206/323-1525. Bus: 10, 11, 49. Map p 129.*

Madison Pub CAPITOL HILL
The crowd at this low-key pub is mixed, but mostly gay and male. It's a down-to-earth place with welcoming bartenders. *1315 E. Madison St.* ☎ *206/325-6537. Bus: 2. Map p 129.*

★ **Neighbours** CAPITOL HILL
This longtime favorite disco is gay-friendly but attracts a mixed group to its large dance floor. *1509 Broadway.* ☎ *206/324-5358. Bus: 11, 49. Map p 129.*

★ **Purr** CAPITOL HILL   Catch the rotating exhibits of local artists' works at this comfy, relaxed bar, and sing along with the karaoke crowd on Tuesdays. It's a mixed, mainly gay clientele. *1518 11th Ave.* ☎ *206/325-3112. Bus: 11, 49. Map p 129.*

Re-bar BELLTOWN   There's always something going on at this funky club, which attracts a mixed straight/younger gay (some in drag) clientele. What's going on might be a band or even live theater—and there's dancing every night. *1114 Howell St.* ☎ *206/233-9873. Map p 128.*

The Wild Rose CAPITOL HILL
Everyone is welcome at Seattle's only real lesbian bar, where the drinks are strong, the bar food is good, and the atmosphere is laid-back. *1021 E. Pike St.* ☎ *206/324-9210. Bus: 11, 49. Map p 129.* ●

Arts & Entertainment **Best Bets**

Most **Jaw-Dropping Show With Dinner**
★★★ Teatro Zinzani, *222 Mercer St. (p 140)*

Best **Place to Go for a Chuckle**
★ The Comedy Underground, *222 Main St. (p 138)*

Best **Family Entertainment**
★★ ZooTunes, *N. 59th St. and Evanston Ave. (p 139)*

Best **Popular Music**
★★★ Showbox, *1426 1st Ave. (p 141)*

Best **Orchestra**
★★★ Seattle Symphony, *200 University St. (p 138)*

Most **Unpredictable Theater Calendar**
★★ The Moore Theatre, *1932 2nd Ave. (p 142)*

Best **Place to Hear Chamber Music One Night and a Talk on Religion or Politics the Next**
★★ Town Hall, *1119 8th Ave. (p 138)*

Best **Theater to Take Your Date Before Proposing**
★★★ Paramount Theatre, *911 Pine St. (p 142)*

Best **Place to Watch an Arabesque**
★★★ Pacific Northwest Ballet, *305 Harrison St. (p 139)*

Most **Eclectic Musical Lineup**
★★★ The Triple Door, *216 Union St. (p 142)*

The Pacific Northwest Ballet.

Downtown Arts & Entertainment

ACT (A Contemporary
Theatre) 4

Can Can 11

The Comedy
Underground 13

Crepe de Paris 7

Dimitriou's Jazz Alley 1

5th Avenue Theatre 6

Mainstage Comedy
and Music Club 16

The Moore Theatre 2

Pacific Northwest Ballet 19

Paramount Theatre 3

The Pink Door Cabaret 12

Seattle Gilbert &
Sullivan Society 17

Seattle Opera 19

Seattle Symphony 8

Showbox 10

Teatro ZinZanni 18

Town Hall 5

The Triple Door 9

UW World Series 15

ZooTunes 14

Arts & Entertainment **A to Z**

Classical Music
★★★ **Seattle Symphony** DOWN-
TOWN   Led by acclaimed conductor
Gerard Schwarz, the 91-person
orchestra is beloved in the community, and has been going strong for
more than a century. The symphony
is known for pushing the envelope
musically and showcasing contemporary as well as classic works. It performs in the beautiful and acoustically
amazing Benaroya Hall. *200 University
St.* ☎ *206/215-4800. www.seattle
symphony.org. Map p 137.*

Comedy Clubs
★ **The Comedy Underground**
PIONEER SQUARE   Comics from
around the country keep the audience
in stitches here every night of the
week. The roster includes winners of
regional comedy contests, late-night
TV guests, and up-and-comers. The
historic club is headquarters for the
annual Seattle International Comedy
Competition. *222 S. Main St.* ☎ *206/
628-0303. Bus: 99. Map p 137.*

★ **Mainstage Comedy and
Music Club** PIKE PLACE MARKET
At Seattle's newest comedy club,
you can linger over a gourmet
dinner while you watch the show.
Some nights are reserved for comedy, others for live music, and 1 day
a week for open mike. The Mainstage launched an annual Seattle
Rhythm and Blues Festival in 2007.
315 1st Ave. N. ☎ *206/217-3700.
Bus: 1, 2, 13, 15, 18. Map p 137.*

Concert Venues
★★ **Town Hall** FIRST HILL   From
chamber music to science lectures
to political discussions, you never
know what you might hear at Town
Hall, Seattle's cultural gathering
place (it's not connected to the city
government). The beautiful Roman-
revival building houses two performance halls. *1119 8th Ave.* ☎ *206/
652-4255. www.townhallseattle.org.
Ticket prices vary; check website.
Bus: 2. Map p 137.*

The Mainstage offers live music and comedy, in addition to dinner.

The Seattle Symphony Orchestra.

★★ **ZooTunes** FREMONT Every summer, the locals head to Woodland Park Zoo to lounge on a grassy meadow and hear weekly concerts by old favorites and hot new groups. You might hear anyone from Art Garfunkel to the Indigo Girls. The concerts start at 6pm, just inside the northern zoo gate. Lots of folks bring picnic baskets and low chairs or towels, but food is also available. You can buy tickets at the zoo, but many concerts sell out, so try the sales website (www.ticketweb.com) in advance. Check the website for the lineup. *N. 59th St. & Evanston Ave.* ☎ *206/548-2500 x1164. www. zoo.org/zootunes. Prices vary but are reasonable; kids 12 & under free. Bus: 16, 44. Map p 137.*

Dance
★★★ **Pacific Northwest Ballet** QUEEN ANNE One of the country's largest and most acclaimed ballet companies, the PNB gives more than 100 performances a year, mostly at the beautiful Marion Oliver McCaw Hall, culminating in the beloved *Nutcracker* over the holidays. *321 Mercer.* ☎ *206/684-7200. Bus: 3, 4, 16. Map p 137.*

★★ **UW World Series** UNIVERSITY DISTRICT The University of Washington brings in world-class dancers, musicians, and other artists from around the globe to perform at Meany Hall on the UW campus. The season runs October through May. *UW Arts Ticket Office: 4001 University Way NE. Meany Hall is on the west side of the UW campus. 15th Ave. NE. & NE. 40th.* ☎ *206/ 543-4880. www.uwworldseries.org. Tickets $32–$45, $20 students. Map p 137.*

Dinner Theatre
★ **Can Can** PIKE PLACE MARKET This avant-garde cabaret venue is for the daring and open-minded—it's on the cutting edge of neo-burlesque. A $9 small-plate menu

The Pacific Northwest Ballet.

Cheap Tickets

If you decide to catch a show in town but don't have tickets, you could go to the theater box office. But first try Ticketwindow, where you can get discounted deals on many local shows, as well as on lake and harbor cruises. There are three locations in Seattle, or you can check online (www.ticketwindowonline.com). But bear in mind that the online option adds a $4.50 service charge. The booths are located at Pike Place Market: 1st Ave. and Pike St. in the Pike Place Market Information Booth; Capitol Hill: Broadway Market (2nd level), 401 Broadway E.; and Pacific Place (4th level), 6th and Pine sts.

is served Tues–Sun, and dinner/show packages are available. Can Can brings in local and national acts, and its house cabaret troupe performs Wednesdays and Sundays. *94 Pike St. ☎ 206/652-0832. www.thecancan. com. Show $5–$10. Bus: 15, 18, 21, 22, 56. Map p 137.*

Crepe de Paris DOWNTOWN
Catch a lively cabaret show with your prix-fixe dinner at this fun, intimate restaurant. On non-show nights, you can choose from an a la carte French menu. Shows change frequently, but you have to call ahead, as there's no website. *1333 5th Ave., Rainier Square. ☎ 206/623-4111. $48 dinner & show; $18–$20 show only. Bus: 2. Map p 137.*

A performer at Teatro ZinZanni.

★★ The Pink Door Cabaret PIKE
PLACE MARKET   There's almost always something out of the ordinary going on here, be it a trapeze artist or an accordion player. But Saturday nights are reserved for a fun and naughty burlesque show, which starts at 11pm and incorporates cross-dressing and elements of striptease. Come earlier and you can enjoy a delicious Italian meal in the dining room before the show. *1919 Post Alley. ☎ 206/443-3241. Cover for burlesque show $12. Bus: 15, 18, 21, 22, 56. Map p 137.*

★★★ Teatro ZinZanni QUEEN
ANNE   Talk about overstimulation! This incredible spectacle of sights and sounds, set inside a huge circus-style tent, is accompanied by a first-class five-course meal by none other than legendary Seattle Chef Tom Douglas. This 3-hour mix of acrobatics, circus acts, cabaret, and comedy must be experienced to be believed. Teatro just moved to gorgeous new quarters across from McCaw Hall. *222 Mercer St. ☎ 206/802-0015. www.zinzanni.com. Tickets $104 Wed–Sun, $120 Sat. Showtimes 6:30pm Wed–Sat, 5:30pm Sun. Bus: 1, 2, 13, 15, 18. Map p 137.*

A performance by the Seattle Opera.

Opera
★ Seattle Gilbert & Sullivan Society
FIRST HILL   This is an amateur group, but it does the Victorian opera writing pair proud. The shows are fun, colorful, and fast-paced. Various venues and ticket prices; check their website. ☎ 206/682-0796. www.pattersong.org. Bus: 1, 2, 13, 15, 18. Map p 137.

★★★ Seattle Opera
QUEEN ANNE   Housed in the elegant Marion Oliver McCaw Hall, this fine company performs contemporary American compositions and traditional European works with panache. *321 Mercer St.* ☎ 206/389-7676. www.seattle opera.org. Bus: 1, 2, 13, 15, 18. Map p 137.

Popular Music
★★★ Showbox
PIKE PLACE MARKET   One of Seattle's premier music clubs, the legendary Showbox has a lot going for it: great bands, elbow room, acoustics, and lots of all-ages shows. (The under-21s have their own section.) Around since 1939, the ballroom has hosted everyone from Duke Ellington to Pearl Jam. There is also a Showbox in the Sodo district. *Market location: 1426 1st Ave. Sodo: 1700 1st Ave. S. Info line for both* ☎ 206/628-3151.

www.showboxonline.com. Ticket prices vary by event; check website. Bus: 15, 18, 21, 22, 56. Map p 137.

Jazz
★★★ Dimitriou's Jazz Alley
BELLTOWN   The lineup of world-class performers at this large, yet somehow intimate, dinner/jazz club never fails to amaze me. *2033 6th Ave.* ☎ 206/441-9729. www.jazz alley.com. Ticket prices vary; check website. Bus: 70. Map p 137.

Dimitriou's Jazz Alley hosts some of jazz's finest acts.

The Triple Door features a broad range of acts.

★★★ The Triple Door

DOWNTOWN   Jazz is just part of the attraction at this hot club, known for its eclectic roster of performers. Its offerings even include chamber music by a group of musicians from the Seattle Symphony (p 138). *216 Union St.* ☎ *206/838-4343. www. tripledoor.com. Ticket prices vary. Bus: 2, 3, 4, 16. Map p 137.*

Theater

★★ ACT (A Contemporary Theatre)

DOWNTOWN   The focus at this energetic venue is on newer plays and playwrights, rather than the classics. *700 Union St.* ☎ *206/ 292-7676. Ticket prices vary. Bus: 10. Map p 137.*

★★★ 5th Avenue Theatre

DOWNTOWN   This elegant Chinese-themed playhouse produces some of the liveliest theater in Seattle, including original and Broadway-bound shows and Broadway musicals. *1308 5th Ave.* ☎ *206/625-1418. www.5thavenue.org. Ticket prices vary. Bus: 2. Map p 137.*

★★ The Moore Theatre

DOWNTOWN   Seattle's oldest theater, the Moore hosts some of its edgier acts. It's always a diverse lineup; you might see anyone from cross-dressing Dame Edna to Ladysmith Black Mambazo—with perhaps a children's play scheduled in between. *1932 2nd Ave.* ☎ *206/467-5510. www.themoore.com. Ticket prices vary. Bus: 70. Map p 137.*

★★★ Paramount Theatre

DOWNTOWN   From Broadway to rock shows, the Paramount offers superb entertainment in a glamorous historic setting. *911 Pine St.* ☎ *206/467-5510. www.the paramount.com. Ticket prices vary. Bus: 11, 12, 49. Map p 137.* ●

A performance of The Women at ACT.

Downtown Lodging

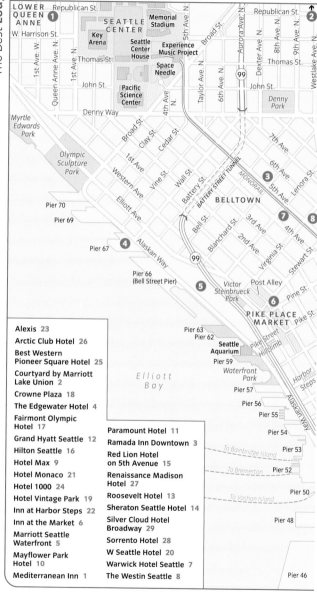

Alexis 23

Arctic Club Hotel 26

Best Western
Pioneer Square Hotel 25

Courtyard by Marriott
Lake Union 2

Crowne Plaza 18

The Edgewater Hotel 4

Fairmont Olympic
Hotel 17

Grand Hyatt Seattle 12

Hilton Seattle 16

Hotel Max 9

Hotel Monaco 21

Hotel 1000 24

Hotel Vintage Park 19

Inn at Harbor Steps 22

Inn at the Market 6

Marriott Seattle
Waterfront 5

Mayflower Park
Hotel 10

Mediterranean Inn 1

Paramount Hotel 11

Ramada Inn Downtown 3

Red Lion Hotel
on 5th Avenue 15

Renaissance Madison
Hotel 27

Roosevelt Hotel 13

Sheraton Seattle Hotel 14

Silver Cloud Hotel
Broadway 29

Sorrento Hotel 28

W Seattle Hotel 20

Warwick Hotel Seattle 7

The Westin Seattle 8

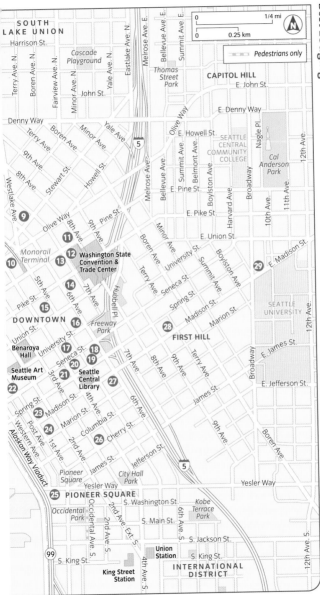

Lodging **Best Bets**

Most **Authentic Seattle Experience**
★★★ The Edgewater Hotel $$$–$$$$ 2411 Alaskan Way (p 147)

Best **Panoramic City Views**
★★★ The Westin Seattle $$$ 1900 5th Ave. (p 152)

Most **Romantic**
★★★ Alexis $$$ 1007 1st Ave. (p 147); and ★★★ Inn at the Market $$$ 86 Pine St. (p 149)

Most **Traditionally Elegant**
★★★ Fairmont Olympic $$$$ 411 University St. (p 147)

Most **Whimsical Fun**
★★★ Hotel Monaco $$$–$$$$ 1101 4th Ave. (p 148)

Most **Elegant European Style**
★★★ Sorrento $$$ 900 Madison St. (p 151)

Most **Intimate**
★★★ Inn at Harbor Steps $$$ 1221 1st Ave. (p 149)

Best **Choice for Wine-Lovers**
★★★ Hotel Vintage Park $$$ 1100 5th Ave. (p 149)

Hippest Hotel
★★★ Hotel 1000 $$$ 1000 1st Ave. (p 148); and ★★★ W Seattle Hotel $$$ 1112 4th Ave. (p 148)

Newest Hot Hotel
★★★ Arctic Club Hotel $$$ 700 3rd Ave. (p 147)

Most **Stunning Lobby**
★★★ Grand Hyatt Seattle $$$ 721 Pine St. (p 148)

Best for **Getting to the Convention Center in the Rain**
★★ Hilton Seattle $$–$$$ 6th Ave. (p 148)

Artsiest Hotel
★★ Hotel Max $$ 620 Stewart St. (p 148)

Best **Bargain**
★★★ Sheraton Seattle Hotel $$ 1400 6th Ave. (p 151)

The Edgewater Hotel brings Seattle's unique style to each of its guest rooms.

Lodging **A to Z**

★★★ [kids] **Alexis** DOWNTOWN
Located just north of Pioneer Square,
this cozy boutique hotel is luxurious
and romantic. A recent $10-million
renovation added 300-thread count
sheets, feather beds, flatscreen TVs,
and a spa. Jetted tubs and wood-
burning fireplaces are available in
some suites, and you can dine at the
charming Library Bistro & Bookstore
Bar. *1007 1st Ave., at Madison.*
☎ *888/850-1155 or 206/624-4844.*
www.alexishotel.com. 121 units.
Double $203–$279. AE, DISC, MC, V.
Bus: 12, 15, 16. Map p 144.

★★★ **Arctic Club Hotel** DOWN-
TOWN This brand-new luxury hotel
is located in a renovated historic
building that once housed an exclusive club for gold prospectors who
had struck it rich. The glamour will
remain, and much history is being
preserved, including sculpted walrus
heads that wrap around the outside
of the building, and beautiful Alaskan
marble. *700 3rd Ave., at Cherry St.*
☎ *800/600-7775 or 206/340-0340.*
www.arcticclubhotel.com. 120 units.
Double $216–$219. Bus: 1, 2, 3, 13,
16. Map p 144.

★ **Best Western Pioneer
Square Hotel** PIONEER SQUARE
Set in the midst of Seattle's charming
historic district, this hotel, housed in
a century-old Romanesque Victorian
building, has loads of quiet charm.
77 Yesler Way. ☎ *800/800-5514 or*
206/340-1234. www.pioneersquare.
com. 72 units. Double $159–$219
w/deluxe continental breakfast. AE,
DISC, MC, V. Bus: 16, 99. Map p 144.

★ [kids] **Courtyard by Marriott
Lake Union** LAKE UNION This
hotel on Lake Union is not in the
heart of downtown, but a nearby
streetcar runs there every 15 minutes until 9pm Mon–Thurs, 11pm

Fri–Sat, and 7pm Sun, and costs a
mere $1.75. The hotel also has a
pool. *925 Westlake Ave. N.* ☎ *800/*
321-2211 or 206/213-0100. www.
courtyardlakeunion.com. 250 units.
Double $169–$229. AE, DC, DISC,
MC, V. Map p 144.

★ **Crowne Plaza** DOWNTOWN
Two blocks from the convention
center and a few blocks from Pike
Place Market, this comfortable,
inviting hotel is also near the
theaters and downtown shops.
1113 6th Ave. ☎ *800/770-5675 or*
206/464-1980. www.cphotelsseattle.
com. 415 units. Double $171–$279.
AE, DC, DISC, MC, V. Bus: 2. Map
p 144.

★★★ **The Edgewater Hotel**
WATERFRONT A landmark Seattle
inn with the woodsy feel of a mountain lodge, it's the only hotel directly
on the waterfront. Perched over
Elliott Bay, the Edgewater affords
stunning sunset views. The Beatles
once stayed here, fishing in the
Sound from their window. *2411
Alaskan Way, Pier 67.* ☎ *800/*
624-0670 or 206/728-7000.
www.edgewaterhotel.com. 223
rooms. Double $259–$409. AE, DC,
DISC, MC, V. Bus: 99. Map p 144.

★★★ [kids] **Fairmont Olympic
Hotel** DOWNTOWN Traditional
elegance is the theme at this classic
luxury hotel. The rooms have down
pillows and duvets and come with
PlayStations. *411 University St.*
☎ *800/257-7544 or 206/621-1700.*
www.fairmont.com/seattle. 450
units. Double $299–$469. MC, V.
Bus: 2. Map p 144.

★★★ **Grand Hyatt Seattle**
DOWNTOWN This high-tech hotel
has comfy beds and oversize bathrooms with soaking tubs. Check out

The lushly elegant lobby at the Fairmont Olympic (p 147).

the local art throughout the hotel, including a glass "waterfall" sculpture in the lobby. And if you don't feel like venturing out for dinner, it's adjacent to Ruth's Chris Steak House. *721 Pine St.* ☎ *888/591-1234 or 206/774-1234. www.grandseattle. hyatt.com. Double $245–$299. AE, DC, DISC, MC, V. Bus: 10, 11, 12, 49. Map p 144.*

★★ **Hilton Seattle** DOWNTOWN Conveniently connected by tunnel to both the convention center and the 5th Avenue shopping area, the Hilton is especially popular with business travelers. The rooms have great views, and they come with large HDTVs. *6th Ave.* ☎ *800/HILTONS or 206/624-0500. www.seattlehilton. com. Double $184–$239. AE, DISC, MC, V. Bus: 2. Map p 144.*

★★ **Hotel Max** DOWNTOWN Don't have time to stop at the art museum? At this unique hotel, where you can choose from a menu of pillow choices, the original works of hundreds of local artists and photographers are showcased in the lobby and guest rooms. There's a sushi (and more) restaurant, the Red Fin, on-site. *620 Stewart St.,* at 6th Ave. ☎ *866/833-6299 or 206/ 728-6299. www.hotelmaxseattle.com. 163 units. Double $143–$159. AE, DISC, MC, V. Monorail or bus 70. Map p 144.*

★★★ **kids** **Hotel Monaco** DOWN-TOWN The colorful, whimsical decor at this lovely boutique hotel makes it an inviting place for kids and adults alike. Kids get their own welcome gift, and Guitar Hero III is available on Fridays. There's plenty of pampering for grown-ups, too, including evening wine receptions. Oh yes, and a fortune-teller on Wednesdays and Saturdays. You can bring your dog—or borrow a gold-fish overnight. And the Sazerac restaurant injects a delightful touch of New Orleans to its dishes. *1101 4th Ave.* ☎ *800/715-6513 or 206/ 621-1770. www.monaco-seattle.com. 189 units. Double $279–$345. AE, DISC, MC, V. Bus: 2. Map p 144.*

★★★ **Hotel 1000** DOWNTOWN This modern, sophisticated hotel offers sleek beauty and the latest in technology (namely, 40-inch flat-screen TVs, free Wi-Fi everywhere). Guest rooms have customizable electronic art, and check out the tubs: They fill from the ceiling down. The technology is impressive, but excellent, friendly service is also part of the mix here. The BOKA Kitchen + Bar offers creative cuisine and a lively lounge scene. *1000 1st Ave.* ☎ *877/315-1088 or 206/957-1000. www.hotel1000seattle.com. 120 units. Double $250–$425. AE, DISC, MC, V. Bus: 15, 18, 21, 22, 56. Map p 144.*

★★★ Hotel Vintage Park DOWNTOWN
A lush, jewel-tone decor tips guests off to the fact that they will be treated like royalty here. In-room spa services are available, and an elegant wine reception showcasing Washington vineyards is held nightly. Each room is dedicated to a Washington winery. Dine at the wonderful Tulio Ristorante. The 5th Avenue Theatre and shops are steps away. Added bonus: soundproof windows. *1100 5th Ave.* ☎ *800/853-3914 or 206/624-8000. www.hotelvintagepark. com. 125 units. Double $219–$299. AE, DISC, MC, V. Bus: 2. Map p 144.*

★★★ Inn at Harbor Steps
DOWNTOWN   Look for the fountain and the gleaming steps leading down to the waterfront and you'll spot this cozy, charming boutique inn across from the Seattle Art Museum. The decor is warm and inviting; most rooms have a fireplace and garden view. Enjoy the swimming pool and complimentary breakfast. Afternoon wine and hors d'oeuvres are included. *1221 1st Ave.* ☎ *888/728-8910 or 206/748-0973. www.innatharborsteps. com. 20 units. Double $200–$210 w/full breakfast. AE, DISC, MC, V. Bus: 10, 12, 15, 18, 21. Map p 144.*

★★★ Inn at the Market PIKE
PLACE MARKET   A romantic hideaway right across from Pike Place Market, this friendly hotel offers spectacular views of Elliott Bay and the mountains. It's a relaxing haven where guests can enjoy morning coffee in the rooftop garden while watching market merchants set up their stalls. The comfy beds are Tempur-Pedic, and room service is from the wonderful Café Campagne. *86 Pine St.* ☎ *800/446-4484 or 206/923-8178. www.innatthe market.com. 70 units. Double $220–$290. AE, DISC, MC, V. Bus: 10, 12, 15, 18, 21. Map p 144.*

The cozy Hotel Monaco is pet-friendly, so bring Fido.

The Best Lodging

★★★ Marriott Seattle Waterfront
WATERFRONT   A short walk from Pike Place Market and across the street from the waterfront, this newer hotel was built with views in mind: water, cityscape, mountains. Half the rooms have balconies. The Marriott is filled with spectacular works by local glass artists. *2100 Alaskan Way.* ☎ *800/455-8254 or 206/443-5000. www.marriott.com/ hotels/travel/seawf-seattle-marriott-waterfront. 358 units. Double $269–$299. AE, DC, DISC, MC, V. Bus: 99. Map p 144.*

★★ Mayflower Park Hotel
DOWNTOWN   This elegantly restored grand dame has been operating since 1927. A wine reception is served Wednesdays at 4:30pm, and the rooms have lots of modern touches. The hotel connects to Westlake Center shopping mall and the monorail. Oliver's Lounge and Andaluca Restaurant are located here. *405 Olive Way.* ☎ *800/426-5100 or 206/623-8700. www. mayflowerpark.com. 171 units.*

The Inn at the Market (p 149) has one of the best locations in town.

Double $225. AE, DC, DISC, MC, V. Monorail. Map p 144.

★ Mediterranean Inn
QUEEN ANNE   A sunny yellow building in a quiet neighborhood houses this moderately priced hotel where rooms come with kitchenettes. It's not close to downtown or the waterfront, but a short stroll takes you to Seattle Center, where you can catch the monorail downtown. *425 Queen Anne Ave. N.* ☎ *866/ 525-4700 or 206/428-4700. www. mediterranean-inn.com. Double $149–$199. AE, DC, DISC, MC, V. Monorail. Map p 144.*

Paramount Hotel
DOWNTOWN   Across the street from the Paramount Theatre, this European-style hotel is also near the convention center and Pacific Place. Among the amenities at this spot: HBO and video games. *724 Pine St.* ☎ *800/ 663-1144 or 206/292-9500. www. paramounthotelseattle.com. 146 units. Double $179–$239. AE, DISC, MC, V. Bus: 10, 11, 12, 49. Map p 144.*

Ramada Inn Downtown
DOWNTOWN   With views of the Space Needle and the downtown cityscape, this is a reasonably priced choice. While not right in the heart of the shopping core, it's just a few blocks away, and within the free bus zone. The on-site Max's Café serves breakfast and lunch. *2200 5th Ave., at Blanchard St.* ☎ *800/272-6232 or 206/441-9785. www.ramada.com. Double $99–$159. AE, DC, DISC, MC, V. Bus: 26, 28, 358. Map p 144.*

★ Red Lion Hotel on 5th Avenue
DOWNTOWN   The Red Lion's location is just about perfect—it's an easy walk from Pike Place Market and the downtown shops—and the rooms aren't bad, either. There's an outdoor dining patio and a pub downstairs. *1415 5th Ave.* ☎ *206/971-8000. www.redlion5th avenue.com. 297 units. Double*

$189–$239. AE, DC, DISC, MC, V. Bus: 10. Map p 144.

★★★ Renaissance Madison Hotel DOWNTOWN

This luxury property offers great views and homey Northwestern decor. The on-site Maxwells serves breakfast, lunch, and dinner. *515 Madison St.* ☎ *800/546-9184 or 206/583-0300. www.marriott.com/hotels/travel/ seasm-renaissance-seattle-hotel. 553 units. Double $219–$300. AE, DISC, MC, V. Bus: 10, 12. Map p 144.*

★ Roosevelt Hotel DOWNTOWN

A lovely old hotel with personality to spare, it's right across from Pacific Place, in the heart of downtown. Don't miss the martinis at Von's Grand City Café, attached to the hotel. *1531 7th Ave.* ☎ *206/621-1200. www.roosevelthotel.com. 151 units. Double $189–$269. AE, DC, DISC, MC, V. Bus: 11, 12, 49. Map p 144.*

★★★ kids Sheraton Seattle Hotel DOWNTOWN

One of the city's largest hotels, the Sheraton has a pool and workout center. Near the convention center and down-town shops, it offers both views and convenience. The beds are oh-so-comfy, and cribs and video games are available for those traveling with kids. *1400 6th Ave.* ☎ *800/325-3535 or 206/621-9000. www.starwood hotels.com/sheraton/seattle. 1,258 units. Double $129–$199. AE, DC, DISC, MC, V. Bus: 10. Map p 144.*

★★ Silver Cloud Hotel Broadway CAPITOL HILL

Situated in the funky Capitol Hill district, the hip Silver Cloud has its own indoor pool and fitness center. A shuttle gets you downtown. *1100 Broadway.* ☎ *800/590-1801 or 206/325-1400 www.silvercloud.com/14home.htm. 179 units. Double $179–$199 w/breakfast. AE, DC, DISC, MC, V. Bus: 12. Map p 144.*

Relax in the lobby of the W after a long day of sightseeing.

★★★ Sorrento Hotel FIRST HILL

This luxury boutique's first guest was Teddy Roosevelt, and it's been pampering travelers with European style and service ever since. Spacious bathrooms feature Italian marble, and rooms come with thoughtful extras like a French press for coffee. The hotel is located in a quiet neighborhood atop a hill and you can either walk downtown or take advantage of the hotel's free town car service. The Fireside Room serves up great drinks and jazz; the Hunt Club is one of Seattle's finest restaurants. *900 Madison St. (at Terry).* ☎ *800/426-1265 or 206/ 622-6400. www.hotelsorrento.com. 76 units. Double $209–$249. AE, MC, V. Bus: 12. Map p 144.*

★★★ W Seattle Hotel DOWNTOWN

Sleek, contemporary, and youthful, the W is trendy in a great way. The rooms are warmly inviting, and you can choose from a "Wonderful" room to an "Extreme Wow" suite (on the 24th floor, with more than 1,000 sq. ft./90 sq. m of space). All have cozy goose-down duvets and down pillows. Get a shi-atsu massage in your room—or most anything (legal!) your heart desires, via the Whatever/Whenever service. The W is also home to the palate-pleasing Earth & Ocean. *1112 4th Ave. ☎ 206/264-6000. http://whotels. com/Seattle. 417 units. Double $253–$331. AE, MC, V. Bus: 2. Map p 144.*

★★ Warwick Hotel Seattle

BELLTOWN   This moderately priced, French-owned property is in Bell-town, an easy walk from downtown and Pike Place Market. It features an indoor pool, accommodating staff, and a balcony on each room. If you don't feel like heading back out for dinner after a long day of sight-seeing, try the hotel's excellent Brasserie Margaux. *401 Lenora St. ☎ 206/443-4300. www.warwickwa. com. 230 units. Double $119–$220.*

AE, DISC, MC, V. Monorail or bus 70. Map p 144.

★★★ kids The Westin Seattle

DOWNTOWN   Located in landmark round towers, the 47-story Westin offers breathtaking views of the Space Needle, Puget Sound, and cityscape. Rooms come with the Westin Heavenly Bed that makes you want to stay in bed a little longer in the morning. Kids get a special welcome kit, and you can request a Heavenly Crib for the baby. Cool off in the roomy indoor pool; enjoy outstanding regional cuisine at the Coldwater Bar and Grill and breakfast or lunch at the Fifth Avenue Corner Cafe. *1900 5th Ave. ☎ 800/WESTIN or 206/728-1000. www.westin.com/seattle. 891 units. Double $199–$280. AE, DISC, V. Monorail or bus 70. Map p 144.* ●

Check out the Space Needle from your room—views from the Westin are spectacular.

Tacoma

1. Tacoma Art Museum
2. Untitled
3. Tacoma Union Station
4. Washington State History Museum
5. Chihuly Bridge of Glass
6. Museum of Glass
7. Point Defiance Zoo & Aquarium

T hirty miles (48km) south of its glitzy northern neighbor, the city of Tacoma has suffered a bit of "ugly stepsister" syndrome over the years. True, it has no Space Needle, but Tacoma has lately spruced up its image by redeveloping its downtown into a charming area with free light rail, an esplanade along the Thea Foss Waterway, and major cultural facilities. A onetime industrial zone is being transformed into a gem of a destination that's definitely worth checking out. START: **Your best bet is to rent a car and drive. Take I-5 South to I-705 North, and use exit 133 to reach the city center. Most of the stops on this tour are within walking distance of each other.**

1 ★★ Tacoma Art Museum. This building is itself a work of art, with a ramp spiraling up through the galleries, which are arranged around an atrium. The museum houses a fine collection of works by Northwest artists, including the world's largest collection of Tacoma native Dale Chihuly's glass.

In addition to American art, you'll find European and Asian works. ⏱ 1 hr. 1701 Pacific Ave. ☎ 253/272-4258. www.tacomaartmuseum. org. Admission $7.50 adults, $6.50 seniors & students, 3rd Thurs of every month free. Tues–Sat 10am–5pm; Sun noon–5pm; 3rd Thurs of every month 10am–8pm.

2 **Untitled.** The stylish cafe at the Tacoma Art Museum is a great place to fuel up before continuing your explorations of Tacoma. Simple but tasty sandwiches, salads, wraps, and soups are served here, along with Pacific Northwest wines. *1701 Pacific Ave. $.*

3 **Tacoma Union Station.** The former terminus of the Northern Pacific Railroad, this grand station was abandoned for many years, then renovated in the 1990s and connected to a new courthouse. There are no more trains, but it's worth a stop to admire the white marble walls and magnificent 90-foot-tall (27m) rotunda dome, now decorated with a splendid 20-foot (6m) Chihuly chandelier. ⏱ *15 min. 1717 Pacific Ave.* ☎ *253/863-5173, ext. 223. Free admission. Mon–Fri 8am–5pm.*

4 ★★★ **kids** **Washington State History Museum.** History comes to life here via high-tech interactive displays. Engaging for all ages, these exhibits make learning history not only painless but terrific fun. "Meet" characters from Washington's past—like Lewis & Clark—in the Great Hall of Washington history. ⏱ *90 min. 1911 Pacific Ave.* ☎ *253/272-3500. Admission $8 adults, $7 seniors, $6 ages 6–17, free for those under 6, $25 family pass, free admission Thurs 5–8pm. Mon–Sat 10am–5pm; Thurs 10am–8pm; Sun noon–5pm.*

5 ★★★ **Chihuly Bridge of Glass.** Connecting the revitalized downtown to Tacoma's waterfront is a spectacular 500-foot (152m) walking bridge by artist Dale Chihuly. It rises 70 feet (21m) into the air as it crosses Interstate 705, and features a ceiling of "seaform" glass, blue crystal towers, and a Venetian wall, containing a variety of glass sculptures.

6 ★★ **Museum of Glass.** Here you'll find works by world-famous contemporary glass artists, including both indoor and outdoor installations. Do not miss stopping in at the museum's Hot Shop, where you can watch glassmakers at work. Best of all, the museum's store features works created on-site. ⏱ *1hr. 1801 Dock St.* ☎ *253/284-4750. www. museumofglass.org. Admission $10 adults, $8 seniors, $4 ages 6–12, free for those under 6, $30 family pass. Summer Wed–Sat 10am–5pm; Sun noon–5pm; 3rd Thurs of every month 10am–8pm. Fall/Winter Wed–Sat 10am–5pm; Sun noon–5pm; 3rd Thurs of every month 10am–8pm.*

7 ★★ **Point Defiance Zoo & Aquarium.** This terrific little zoo is best known for its marine exhibits, including its entertaining beluga whales. I once saw one retrieve a piece of litter thrown in its tank by a guest and deliver it to a docent. ⏱ *90 min. 5400 N. Pearl St.* ☎ *253/ 404-3678. Admission $11 adults, $10 seniors, $9 ages 5–12, $5 ages 3–4. Daily 9am, closing hours vary (check website—www.pdza.org).*

World-famous glass artist Dale Chihuly designed the glass bridge that now connects downtown to the waterfront.

San Juan Islands

1. Friday Harbor Ferry Dock
2. Whale Watch
3. Pelindaba Lavender Gallery
4. The Sweet Retreat and Espresso
5. Whale Museum

Though they're located just a few hours from Seattle, these small islands feel much, much farther away. The quaint portside town of Friday Harbor, at the tip of San Juan Island, is lined with interesting shops, art galleries, and cafes. The islands are a popular getaway for both tourists and local residents. You won't need a car, unless you're dead-set on driving around the islands and doing some exploring. Otherwise, I recommend that you rent bikes or mopeds when you get there. START: **Seattle waterfront or the Anacortes ferry dock.**

---

1 kids Friday Harbor Ferry Dock. This landing, with its stunning views of the surrounding hilly islands, is where your adventure begins. You can get here from the Seattle waterfront, via the Victoria Clipper, or you can drive up I-5 to Anacortes (about a 2-hr. trip), then follow the signs to the Washington State ferry dock. You can take your car on the boat, but it costs quite a bit more. Long-term parking at the dock is cheaper, and you can walk

right onto the boat, whereas car lines can get very long, especially in the summertime. For Anacortes–San Juan Islands ferry schedules, check the website (www.wsdot.wa.gov/ferries). This 90-minute ferry ride is arguably the prettiest in the world, winding its way among enchanting emerald islands. It's spectacular on a sunny day, but dreamy in the mist as well. ⏲ *2 hr each way on Victoria Clipper from Seattle.* ☎ *206/448-5000. www.victoriaclipper.com. Round-trip* fare $75 adults, $38 children, discounts if purchased in advance. By car, 2 hr. to the ferry dock, then 90 min., excluding wait time, each way on the Washington State ferry. Round-trip fares from Anacortes–Friday Harbor for passengers only $11 adults, $5.45 seniors, $8.80 ages 6–18, free for children under 6. For cars under 20 ft. (6m) long, add $38, which includes driver's fare.

② ★★★ kids Whale Watch.
A number of whale-watch cruises leave from Friday Harbor. If you get there via the Victoria Clipper, whale-watch tickets can be purchased as part of a package deal. Most companies won't guarantee you'll see sleek black-and-white orcas leaping out of the water, but the odds that you will are pretty good in the summer. Most boats have knowledgeable guides who are able to recognize the individual whales in the resident pods. ⏱ 2½ hr. from Friday Harbor Port. Victoria Clipper ☎ 800/888-2535. www.clippervacations.com. Prices vary, depending on date, how far in advance tickets are purchased & whether purchased separately or as package from Seattle. Victoria Clipper whale-watch-only fares $40 adults, $20 ages 1–11.

③ ★ Pelindaba Lavender Gallery.
Who knew there were so many uses for lavender—from cooking ingredients to pet-odor spray? Pelindaba grows its own lavender right on San Juan Island. In fact, you can even drive out to the farm and wander through the fields—all they ask is that you close the gates behind you. ⏱ 20 min. Gallery: 150 1st St., Friday Harbor. ☎ 360/378-6900. www.pelindabalavender.com. Daily 9am–5pm. Farm: Wold Rd., Friday Harbor. Open daily dawn–dusk.

④ If the salt air has you longing
for something cool and sweet, beat a path to **The Sweet Retreat and Espresso,** just a couple blocks from the ferry dock. Housed in a charming stand with flower boxes, you can grab yourself a snack and settle onto a bench along the waterfront. Owner Kathie Morton makes exceptional hand-dipped ice cream, fruit smoothies, and granitas, among other things. If you want something a bit more substantial, try one of her homemade soups or chili. 264 Spring St. ☎ 360/378-1957. $.

⑤ ★ Whale Museum.
Three blocks from the harbor, this unusual little museum is chock-full of information on these huge sea mammals, especially the three orca pods that spend their summers around the San Juans. Exhibits include a whale skeleton. ⏱ 1 hr. 62 1st St. N. ☎ 360/378-4710. www.whalemuseum.org. $6 adults, $5 seniors, $3 students & children 5–18, free for children under 5. Daily 10am–5pm.

Watch for the lighthouse as you head out to find whales.

Mount Rainier National Park

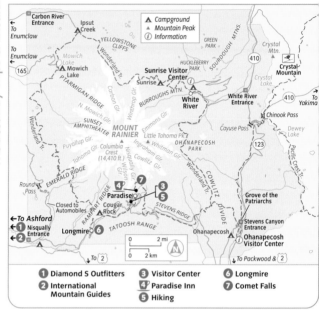

Legend:
▲ Campground
▲ Mountain Peak
ⓘ Information

Map labels:
Carbon River Entrance
To Enumclaw
Ipsut Creek
YELLOWSTONE CLIFFS
Mowich Lake
To Enumclaw
165
Mowich Lake
PTARMIGAN RIDGE
N. Mowich Glr.
Wonderland Tr.
Carbon Glr.
Winthrop Glr.
GREEN PARK
Crystal Mtn.
410
HUCKLEBERRY PARK
SOURDOUGH MTNS.
Sunrise Visitor Center
Sunrise
BURROUGHS MTN
White River
Crystal Mountain
Crystal Lake
White River Entrance
410
To Yakima
Chinook Pass
SUNSET AMPHITHEATER
MOUNT RAINIER
Little Tahoma Pk.
Emmons Glr.
Whitman Glr.
Ingraham Glr.
OHANAPECOSH PARK
Cayuse Pass
Dewey Lake
123
Puyallup Glr.
Tahoma Glr.
Columbia Crest (14,410 ft.)
Nisqually Glr.
Cowlitz Glr.
Wilson Glr.
Wonderland Tr.
Pacific Crest Tr.
EMERALD RIDGE
Round Pass
Wonderland Tr.
Paradise
Closed to Automobiles
Cougar Rock
RAMPART RIDGE
STEVENS RIDGE
COWLITZ DIVIDE
Grove of the Patriarchs
←To Ashford
1 Nisqually Entrance
2
Longmire
TATOOSH RANGE
Ohanapecosh
Stevens Canyon Entrance
Ohanapecosh Visitor Center
0   2 mi
0   2 km
↓ To 2
↓ To Packwood & 2

1 Diamond S Outfitters
2 International Mountain Guides
3 Visitor Center
4 Paradise Inn
5 Hiking
6 Longmire
7 Comet Falls

Seattleites can go for weeks without seeing the sun, and they're pretty okay with that. What gets them down is when the gray skies blanket their beloved Mount Rainier, which soars a mile-and-a-half (2.4km) above the surrounding Cascade peaks. When it breaks through the clouds, you'll no doubt hear someone gleefully say, "The mountain's out!" Less than 3 hours from the city, Mt. Rainier is considered something of a backyard by Seattleites, who love to hike it, climb it, picnic on it, and marvel at its wildflowers. START: **Plan to rent a car and head south on I-5 to I-405 North. Merge with Rte. 167 South and follow signs for the park.**

1 ★★ **Saddle Up.** Take a 2-hour guided horse ride just outside the national park at Diamond S Outfitters. They have excellent guides and miles of trails to explore. Don't worry if you've never ridden a horse before—no experience is necessary. Just be sure to make a reservation 2–3 days in advance, as slots fill up quickly. ⏱ *2 hr. 27913 549th St. E.,* Ashford. ☎ *360/569-2033. www.diamondsoutfitters.com. Ages 6 & up. Rides $60 per person. Open May–Sept.*

2 ★ **Go Climbing.** Several mountain-climbing organizations offer programs for various levels of climbers (including novices). I suggest you try International Mountain

Guides, which leads a wide-range of climbs and hikes. *31111 S.R. 706 E., Ashford.* ☎ *360/569-2609. www.mountainguides.com. Prices start at $172 for a 1-day moun-taineering course.*

❸ Visitor Center. The Nisqually Entrance of Mount Rainier National Park is open year-round, as is the ride along the Nisqually–Paradise Road to Paradise. The drive is spectacular, winding through old-growth forest as the road climbs the mountain. At Paradise, stop at the Visitor Center for maps of the park and its many trails. Free nature walks also leave from the center. ☎ *360/569-2211, ext. 2328.*

❹ The stunning Paradise Inn, a national historic building constructed from Alaskan cedar, is newly renovated and worth a stop. It's a beautiful spot with a huge fireplace and the cozy feel of a backwoods lodge. You can grab a bowl of chili and a blackberry cobbler, or go for something more substantial. ☎ *360/569-2275. $.*

❺ ★★★ Take a Hike. The park maps will help you decide which trails best suit your needs, and feel free to ask the friendly rangers at the Visitor Center for advice. There are plenty of easy hikes, and lots of tougher ones as well. You'll be treated to dramatic mountain vistas, and, if you're lucky, some wildlife. If you're not in the mood for exercise, continue driving up the Nisqually–Paradise Road to Kautz Creek, where you can park and enjoy the view of Mount Rainier. If you decide you want to stretch your legs, you can also hike along the Kautz Creek trail to Indian Henry's Hunting Ground.

❻ Longmire. Nisqually–Paradise Road takes you next to Longmire, where you will find a museum with exhibits about the land's history and geology, as well as the National Park Inn (☎ 360/569-2275) and more trails near mineral springs.

❼ ★ Comet Falls. About 10 miles (16km) from the entrance to the park, Niqually–Paradise Road takes you to a 300-foot (91m) waterfall, Comet Falls. You can hike there or drive to the viewing area, just past Christine Falls.

A view of Mt. Rainier.

Vancouver, BC

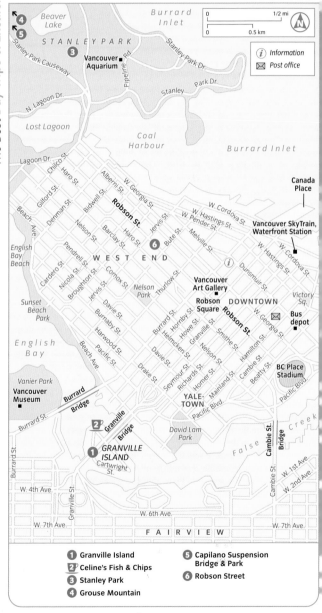

1 Granville Island
2 Celine's Fish & Chips
3 Stanley Park
4 Grouse Mountain
5 Capilano Suspension Bridge & Park
6 Robson Street

So close to Seattle it's considered a neighbor, Vancouver is a sophisticated city with lots to offer travelers of all ages and interests. The people are friendly, the shopping and dining top-notch, the skyline dramatic. Set on the Pacific Ocean, with the majestic Coast Mountains looming in the background, this is breathtaking country. To get there, you can either drive or take the Amtrak Cascades, a 4-hour ride through gorgeous country (☎ 800/USA-RAIL; www.amtrak.com). Either way, remember that passports are a must. And be aware that Vancouver knows how to do public transportation, so getting around town is a breeze whether you use the light rail (the Vancouver Sky Train), bus, or ferry. START: **Rent a car and drive north on I-5 from Seattle, or leave from the Amtrak station at 303 S. Jackson St.**

❶ ★★★ Granville Island. If you have time for only one stop, make it lively, picturesque Granville Island. The Public Market is an almost over-whelming sensory experience of colors, smells, and tastes. (Take advantage of the free samples!) The fish and produce are fresh and delicious. Meanwhile, entertainers of one sort or another are almost always performing on the deck. Shops range from custom-made jewelry to magic kits. To get to the island, take the #50 False Creek bus from Gastown (downtown area), which stops just off Granville Island; walk toward the sign. Other city buses will take you to Granville & 5th Ave., and you can walk to the island. You can also take a ferry (continuous runs 7am–10:30pm in the summer, until 8:30pm in the winter).

❷ Celine's Fish & Chips. The salt air always puts me in the mood for seafood. You can grab a great salmon burger at Celine's, in the Public Market, then head outdoors on the deck to munch while you enjoy the entertainment. *1689 Johnston St. #109.* ☎ *604/669-8650.*

The Public Market at Granville Island rivals Pike Place Market.

❸ ★★★ kids Stanley Park. One of the most magnificent urban parks in the world, Stanley is a 1,000-acre (400-hectare) paradise of meadows, forests, and gardens. As if the natural beauty weren't enough, there's plenty to do here. The Vancouver Aquarium is open daily. The Variety for Kids Water Park is free and open from May until Labor Day. A children's farm (☎ 604/257-8530) and miniature train ride delight children (check the website for current schedule: www.city.vancouver.bc.ca/parks/parks/stanley/fun.htm). The #19 bus will take you to Stanley Park from downtown. Once there, you can take a free shuttle around the park from 10am to 6pm, mid-June

The Best Day Trips & Excursions

Stanley is considered one of the world's great urban parks—and it's easy to see why.

through late September. It stops at 15 attractions within the park. Or hire a horse-and-carriage and go in style. ⏱ *2 hr. Georgia St., north end.* ☎ *604/257-8400. Vancouver Aquarium* ☎ *604/659-3474. www.van aqua.org. Admission $20 adults, $12 ages 4–12, free for children under 4. Summer daily 9:30am–7pm; winter daily 9:30am–5pm).*

④ ★ Grouse Mountain. Just a 15-minute drive from the city, Grouse Mountain is fun any time of year. In the winter, there's snowshoeing, ice-skating, and sleigh rides. In the summer, take the SkyRide cable car ($24 adults, $17 ages 13–18, $9 ages 5–12, free for children under 5) up to the top and enjoy the panoramic view. You can also watch interesting films about endangered animals and eat at the Observatory Restaurant. ⏱ *2 hr. 6400 Nancy Greene Way.* ☎ *604/980-9311. Take Bus 232 from Phibbs Exchange or Bus 236 from Lonsdale Quay. Or drive north across Lions Gate Bridge, take the North Vancouver exit to Marine Dr., then 3 miles (5km) up Capilano Rd. Daily 9am–10pm.*

⑤ ★★ Capilano Suspension Bridge & Park. This 443-foot (135m) swinging bridge gives you a breathtaking view of the rainforest and the Capilano River rushing along below. In the park, you can watch First Nation carving demonstrations and go on the Treetops Adventure, which takes you far above the forest floor on a series of suspension bridges. ⏱ *90 min.* ☎ *604/985-7474. www.capbridge.com. Mar–May 16 admission $27 adults, $16 ages 13–16, $8.30 ages 6–12, free for children under 6; May 17–Oct 31 admission $28 adults, $17 ages 13–16, $8.75 ages 6–12, free for children under 6.*

⑥ ★ Robson Street. The Rodeo Drive of Vancouver, this is where you'll find upscale shops with trend-setting fashion, shoes, and jewelry. It's a fun urban experience, and lots of cafes and coffee shops beckon you to take a break from your shopping. Even if you don't buy anything, the people-watching is great fun. ●

If you're afraid of heights, you may want to skip the Capilano Suspension Bridge, though you should still check out the park.

The
Savvy Traveler

Before You Go

Government Tourist Offices

Need more information about Seattle? You can get all the details your heart desires by contacting **Seattle's Convention and Visitors Bureau,** 701 Pike St., Ste. 800, Seattle, WA 98101 (☎ **206/461-5840;** www.seeseattle.org). The CVB also operates the **Citywide Concierge & Visitor Center** inside the Washington State Convention and Trade Center, Seventh Avenue and Pike Street, main level (☎ **206/461-5888**).

For information on travel to other parts of Washington, contact **Washington State Tourism** (☎ **800/544-1800;** www.experiencewashington.com).

The Best Times to Go

Around the Fourth of July, summer arrives with a bang in Seattle. From then through the end of September, the rain goes away (at least for the most part) and Seattleites come out to play. The picture-perfect weather means hotels and restaurants are crowded, so book as far in advance as possible. If you're not afraid of the rain—despite the city's reputation, it's usually more of a mist than a downpour—come in the winter months, when rates are lower, crowds are thinner, and the theaters are churning out top-notch productions. And with Seattle's temperate climate, it will probably be warmer than wherever you started out.

Festivals & Special Events

SPRING. April brings the **Skagit Valley Tulip Festival** (☎ 360/428-5959; www.tulipfestival.org), in and around La Conner. An hour north of Seattle, acres and acres of tulips and daffodils blanket the Skagit Valley for weeks, accompanied by festivities.

May starts with a splash the first Saturday of the month, **Opening Day of Boating Season** (☎ 206/325-1000; www.seattleyachtclub.org). It's held on Lakes Union and Washington. Next comes the first big street fair, the **U District Street-Fair** (☎ 206/547-4417; www.udistrictstreetfair.org), in the lively University District. Also in mid-May is the **Seattle International Children's Festival** (☎ 206/684-7338; www.seattleinternational.org), at Seattle Center, celebrating cultures from around the world. Then comes the world-famous **Seattle International Film Festival** (☎ 206/324-9996; www.seattlefilm.com), held at area theaters, mid-May through early June. On Memorial Day weekend, the **Northwest Folklife Festival** (☎ 206/684-7300; www.nwfolklife.org), at Seattle Center, honors the many cultures that come together in the Northwest.

SUMMER. The third weekend in June is time for the wackiest festival of all, the **Fremont Fair** (☎ 206/694-6706; www.fremontfair.com), which sees in the summer solstice with a quirky parade, complete with political satire and naked bicyclists. At the end of the month comes **Seattle Pride** (☎ 206/322-9561; www.seattlepride.org), a gay, lesbian, bisexual, and transgender festival.

On the Fourth of July, there are two places to be: either the **Fourth of Jul-Ivar's** (☎ 206/587-6500; www.ivars.net), Myrtle Edwards Park, with fireworks over Elliott Bay; or the **Washington Mutual Family Fourth at Lake Union** (☎ 206/281-7788; www.familyfourth.org), with fireworks over the lake. The biggest event of the season is **Seafair** (☎ 206/728-0123; www.seafair.com), which starts in early July and lasts for a month. Highlights are the hydroplane boat races, the Navy's Blue Angels show, and the Torchlight Parade. At **Bite of Seattle** in mid-July, crowds head to Seattle Center to hear live bands and sample treats and wine from local restaurants.

Wrapping up the summer is **Bumbershoot,** the Seattle Music & Arts Festival (☎ 206/281-7788; www.bumbershoot.org), at Seattle Center on Labor Day weekend. It's a little bit crazy and a lot of fun.

FALL. **Issaquah Salmon Days Festival** (☎ 425/392-0661; www.salmondays.org) welcomes the salmon on their return to the lakes and streams. Issaquah, 15 miles east of Seattle, the first full weekend in October.

WINTER. Throughout December, the **Argosy Cruises Christmas Ships Festival** (☎ 800/642-7816 or 206/623-1445; www.argosycruises.com) takes place at various waterfront locations. Boats decked out with Christmas lights parade past a number of beaches. And what better way to ring in the new year than with **New Year's at the Needle** (☎ 800/937-9582 or 206/905-2100; www.spaceneedle.com), Seattle Center, December 31.

Seattle celebrates the Chinese New Year in a big way, with dragon kites, music, and dance. **The Chinatown/International District Lunar New Year Celebration** (☎ 206/382-1197; www.cidbia.org) takes place near Union Station. In 2009, the Chinese New Year celebration is in late January. The next month, gardening buffs head to the **Northwest Flower & Garden Show** (☎ 206/789-5333; www.gardenshow.com), at the Washington State Convention and Trade Center.

The Weather
Okay, so Seattle doesn't come to mind when you think of sunny destinations. But if you're here in July, August, or September, when those glorious summer days stretch on until 10pm, you might think the city has an undeserved rap. Come back in November. Even then, the rain is generally more drizzle than downpour. When they run the numbers, it turns out that Seattle get 19 inches less rain every year than Miami—though it rains here 29 more days. Theirs is torrential downpour; ours is gentle mist. So Seattle has less rain but more gray days. No matter when you visit Seattle, bring an umbrella or hooded jacket for chilly nights. Winters seldom bring below-freezing temperatures in temperate Seattle, and snow is a rarity in the city.

SEATTLE'S AVERAGE TEMPERATURE & DAYS OF RAIN

	JAN	FEB	MAR	APR	MAY	JUNE
Temp. (°F)	46	50	53	58	65	69
Temp. (°C)	8	10	12	14	18	21
Rain (days)	16	17	14	10	9	5

	JULY	AUG	SEPT	OCT	NOV	DEC
Temp. (°F)	75	74	69	60	52	47
Temp. (°C)	24	23	21	16	11	8
Rain (days)	7	9	14	18	20	19

Useful Websites

- **www.visitseattle.org:** The Seattle Convention and Visitors Bureau has everything you need to know about the city.

- **www.seatac.org/seatac:** Lots of useful information on Seattle's major airport, including real-time flight info.

- **www.seattletimes.com:** The official site of the city's largest paper offers up-to-the-minute Seattle news.

- **www.seattleweekly.com:** The best source for arts and entertainment listings.

- **www.wsdot.wa.gov/ferries:** The spot for ferry pricing and schedules.

Car Rentals

All the major car-rental agencies have offices in Seattle and at or near Seattle-Tacoma International Airport. These include the following:

- **Advantage** (☎ **800/777-5500** or 206/824-0161; www.arac.com)

- **Alamo** (☎ **800/462-5266** or 206/433-0182; www.goalamo.com)

- **Avis** (☎ **800/331-1212** or 206/433-5232; www.avis.com)

- **Budget** (☎ **800/527-0700** or 206/444-7510; www.budget.com)

- **Dollar** (☎ **800/800-4000** or 206/433-5825; www.dollar.com)

- **Enterprise** (☎ **800/261-7331** or 206/246-1953; www.enterprise.com)

- **Hertz** (☎ **800/654-3131** or 206/248-1300; www.hertz.com)

- **National** (☎ **800/227-7368** or 206/433-5501; www.nationalcar.com)

- **Thrifty** (☎ **800/847-4389** or 877/283-0898; www.thrifty.com)

Cellphones

It's a good bet that your phone will work in major cities, but take a look at your wireless company's coverage map on its website before heading out; T-Mobile, Sprint, and Nextel are particularly weak in rural areas. If you need to stay in touch at a destination where you know your phone won't work, rent a phone that does from InTouch USA (☎ 800/872-7626; www.intouchglobal.com) or a rental car location, but beware that you'll pay $1 a minute or more for airtime.

Getting **There**

By Plane

The **Seattle-Tacoma International Airport** (☎ **206/433-5388;** www.portseattle.org/seatac) is served by about 30 airlines.

International carriers that fly from Europe to Los Angeles and/or San Francisco (continue to Seattle on a domestic carrier) include **Aer Lingus** (☎ **0818/365-000** in Ireland; www.aerlingus.com) and **British**

Airways (☎ **0870/850-9850;** www.britishairways.com). The latter also flies directly to Seattle from London.

From New Zealand and Australia, there are flights to San Francisco and Los Angeles on **Qantas** (☎ **13-13-13** in Australia; www.qantas.com.au) and **Air New Zealand** (☎ **0800/737-000** in New Zealand; www.airnewzealand.co.nz).

From Los Angeles, you can continue on to Seattle on a regional domestic carrier.

Seaplane service between Seattle and the San Juan Islands and Victoria, British Columbia, is offered by **Kenmore Air** (☎ 866/435-9524 or 425/486-1257; www.kenmoreair. com), which has its Seattle terminals at the south end of Lake Union and at the north end of Lake Washington.

By Car
There are two main exits from the airport: From the loading/unloading area, take the first exit if you're staying near the airport. Take the second exit (Wash. 518) if you're headed to downtown Seattle. Driving east on Wash. 518 will connect you to I-5, where you'll then follow the signs for Seattle. Generally, allow 30 minutes for the drive between the airport and downtown—45 minutes to an hour during rush hour.

A taxi into downtown Seattle will cost you about $34 to $36 ($28 for the return ride to the airport). There are usually plenty of taxis around, but if not, call **Yellow Cab** (☎ 206/ 622-6500) or **Farwest Taxi** (☎ 206/ 622-1717). The flag-drop charge is $2.50; after that, it's $2 per mile.

Gray Line Airport Express (☎ 800/426-7532 or 206/626-6088; www.graylineofseattle.com) is your best bet for getting downtown. They leave the airport every 30 minutes from 5:30am (5am from downtown) to 11pm. Passengers are picked up outside the baggage-claim area, at Door 00 just past baggage carousel 1. Shuttles stop at the following downtown hotels: Madison Renaissance, Crowne Plaza, Fairmont Olympic, Seattle Hilton, Sheraton Seattle, Grand Hyatt, Westin, and Warwick. Fares are $10 one-way and $17 round-trip for adults and $7.25 one-way and $12 round-trip for children 2–12. Connector service (☎ 206/255-7159) to and from the above hotels is also provided from numerous other downtown hotels, as well as from the Amtrak station, the Washington State Ferries terminal (Pier 52), and the Greyhound station.

Shuttle Express (☎ 800/487-7433 or 425/981-7000; www.shuttle express.com) provides 24-hour service between Sea-Tac and the Seattle, North Seattle, and Bellevue areas. Rates to University District hotels are $32 for one adult, $38 for two adults, $45 for three, and $50 for four. Rates to downtown Seattle are $29 for one or two adults, $33 for three, and $36 for four. Children 12 and under ride free. You need a reservation to get to the airport, but to leave the airport, simply head to the Ground Transportation Center on the third floor of the parking garage.

Metro Transit (☎ 800/542-7876 in Washington, or 206/553-3000; http://transit.metrokc.gov) operates two public buses between the airport and downtown. These buses leave from near Door 6 (close to carousel no. 5) of the baggage-claim area. It's a good idea to call for the current schedule when you arrive in town. Bus no. 194 runs every 15 to 30 minutes; it operates Monday through Friday from about 6am to 9pm, Saturday from about 6:30am to 9pm, and Sunday from about 6:30am to 7:30pm. Bus no. 174 runs every 25 to 30 minutes; it operates Monday through Friday from about 4:50am to 2:45am, Saturday from about 5:20am to 2:45am, and Sunday from about 6:25am to 2:45pm. Bus trips to downtown take 40 to 50 minutes. The fare is $1.25 to $2.

Getting **Around**

By Car

Seattle is 110 miles from Vancouver, British Columbia; 175 miles from Portland; 810 miles from San Francisco; 1,190 miles from Los Angeles; 835 miles from Salt Lake City; and 285 miles from Spokane. I-5 is the main north–south artery, running south to Portland (and then California) and north to the Canadian border. I-405 is Seattle's eastside bypass and accesses Bellevue, Redmond, and Kirkland on the east side of Lake Washington. I-90, which ends at I-5, connects Seattle to Spokane in the eastern part of Washington. Wash. 520 connects I-405 with Seattle just north of downtown and also ends at I-5. Wash. 99, the Alaskan Way Viaduct, is another major north–south highway through downtown Seattle; it passes through the waterfront section of the city. All the major car-rental agencies have offices in Seattle and at or near Seattle-Tacoma International Airport.

Keep in mind that Seattle traffic congestion is bad, parking is limited (and expensive), and streets are almost all one-way. You'll avoid frustration by leaving your car in your hotel parking garage. You might not need a car at all. The city center is well served by public transportation. But if your plans include any excursions out of the city, you'll need a car.

Also bear in mind that on-street parking in downtown Seattle is expensive and extremely limited. Most downtown parking lots charge $20 to $25 per day, though many offer early-bird specials. Some lots near the Space Needle charge less, and you can leave your car there. Some restaurants and Pike Place Market merchants validate parking permits.

By Ferry

Seattle is served by **Washington State Ferries** (☎ 800/843-3779 or 888/808-7977 within Washington, or 206/464-6400; www.wsdot.wa.gov/ferries). Car ferries travel between downtown Seattle and both Bainbridge Island and Bremerton from Pier 52, Colman Dock. Car ferries also connect Fauntleroy (in West Seattle) with Vashon Island and the Kitsap Peninsula at Southworth; Tahlequah (Vashon Island) with Point Defiance in Tacoma; Edmonds with Kingston (on the Kitsap Peninsula); Mukilteo with Whidbey Island; Whidbey Island at Keystone with Port Townsend; and Anacortes with the San Juan Islands and Sidney, British Columbia (on Vancouver Island near Victoria).

If you're traveling between Victoria, British Columbia, and Seattle, several options are available through **Victoria Clipper,** Pier 69, 2701 Alaskan Way (☎ 800/888-2535, 206/448-5000, or 250/382-8100 in Victoria; www.victoriaclipper.com). Ferries make the 2- or 3-hour trip throughout the year, at prices ranging from $79 to $140 round-trip for adults.

By Train

Amtrak (☎ 800/872-7245; www.amtrak.com) service runs from Vancouver, British Columbia, to Seattle and from Portland and as far south as Eugene, Oregon, on the Cascades. The train takes about 4 hours from Vancouver to Seattle and 3½ to 4 hours from Portland to Seattle, assuming there aren't delays (and there often are, especially during the rainy season). One-way fares from Vancouver to Seattle or from Portland to Seattle run $28 to $37. There is also Amtrak service to

Seattle from San Diego, Los Angeles, San Francisco, and Portland on the Coast Starlight, and from Spokane and points east on the Empire Builder. Amtrak also operates a bus between Vancouver and Seattle, so be careful when making a reservation or you won't even be on a train. Go to www.amtrak.com for schedules and pricing.

By Bus

Greyhound (☎ 800/231-2222; www.greyhound.com) bus service provides connections to almost any city in the continental United States. Seattle's Greyhound bus station is at 811 Stewart St. (☎ 206/628-5561), a few blocks northeast of downtown.

Several budget chain motels are located nearby, and you can grab a free ride into downtown on a Metro bus.

In fact, the best thing about Seattle's **Metro** (☎ 800/542-7876 in Washington or 206/553-3000; http://transit.metrokc.gov) bus system is that as long as you stay within the downtown area, you can ride for free between 6am and 7pm. The Ride Free Area is between Alaskan Way (the waterfront) to the west, Sixth Avenue and I-5 to the east, Battery Street to the north, and South Jackson Street to the south. If you travel outside the Ride Free Area, fares range from $1.25 to $2, depending on distance and time of day.

Fast **Facts**

AREA CODE The area code is 206 in Seattle, 425 for the Eastside (including Kirkland and Bellevue), and 253 for south King County (near the airport).

ATMS/CASHPOINTS Nationwide, the easiest and best way to get cash away from home is from an ATM (automated teller machine), sometimes referred to as a "cash machine." The **Cirrus** (☎ 800/424-7787; www.mastercard.com) and **PLUS** (☎ 800/843-7587; www.visa.com) networks span the country.

BABYSITTERS Many Seattle hotels offer babysitting. If not, the concierge should be able to help you find a reliable service.

BUSINESS HOURS The following are general guidelines. Banks are open Monday through Friday from 9am to 5pm (some also on Sat 9am–noon). Stores are open Monday through Saturday from 10am to 6pm and Sunday from noon to 5pm (malls usually stay open until 9pm Mon–Sat). Bars can stay open until 1am.

CONSULATES & EMBASSIES All embassies are located in the nation's capital, Washington, D.C. Some consulates are located in major U.S. cities, and most nations have a mission to the United Nations in New York City. If your country isn't listed below, call for directory information in Washington, D.C. (☎ 202/555-1212) or log on to www.embassy.org/embassies.

The embassy of **Australia** is at 1601 Massachusetts Ave. NW, Washington, DC 20036 (☎ 202/797-3000; www.austemb.org). There are consulates in New York, Honolulu, Houston, Los Angeles, and San Francisco.

The embassy of **Canada** is at 501 Pennsylvania Ave. NW, Washington, DC 20001 (☎ 202/682-1740; www.canadianembassy.org). Other Canadian consulates are in Buffalo (New York), Detroit, Los Angeles, New York, and Seattle.

The embassy of **Ireland** is at 2234 Massachusetts Ave. NW,

Washington, DC 20008 (☎ 202/462-3939; www.irelandemb.org). Irish consulates are in Boston, Chicago, New York, San Francisco, and other cities. See website for complete listing.

The embassy of **New Zealand** is at 37 Observatory Circle NW, Washington, DC 20008 (☎ 202/328-4800; www.nzemb.org). New Zealand consulates are in Los Angeles, Salt Lake City, San Francisco, and Seattle.

The embassy of the **United Kingdom** is at 3100 Massachusetts Ave. NW, Washington, DC 20008 (☎ 202/588-7800; www.britainusa.com). Other British consulates are in Atlanta, Boston, Chicago, Cleveland, Houston, Los Angeles, New York, San Francisco, and Seattle.

DENTIST   Contact the **Dental Referral Service** (☎ 800/510-7315).

DOCTORS   See "Hospitals," below.

ELECTRICITY   The U.S. uses 110 to 120 volts AC (60 cycles). If your appliances use 220 to 240 volts, you'll need a 110-volt transformer and a plug adapter with two flat parallel pins. They're hard to find here, so bring one from home.

EMERGENCIES   For police, fire, or medical emergencies, phone ☎ 911.

EVENT LISTINGS   See "Useful Websites," p 166.

HOLIDAYS   Banks, government offices, post offices, and many stores, restaurants, and museums are closed on the following legal national holidays: January 1 (New Year's Day), the third Monday in January (Martin Luther King, Jr., Day), the third Monday in February (Presidents' Day), the last Monday in May (Memorial Day), July 4 (Independence Day), the first Monday in September (Labor Day), the second Monday in October (Columbus Day), November 11 (Veterans' Day/Armistice Day), the fourth Thursday in November

(Thanksgiving Day), and December 25 (Christmas). The Tuesday after the first Monday in November is Election Day.

HOSPITALS   Hospitals convenient to downtown include **Swedish Medical Center,** 747 Broadway (☎ 206/386-6000; www.swedish.org), and **Virginia Mason Medical Center,** 1100 Ninth Ave. (☎ 206/583-6433 for emergencies or 206/624-1144 for information; www.virginiamason.org).

INTERNET ACCESS   First, ask at your hotel to see if it provides Internet access. Alternatively, you can head to the **Seattle Central Library,** 1000 Fourth Ave. (☎ 206/386-4636), which has hundreds of online computer terminals. And many of Seattle's famed coffeehouses offer free Wi-Fi, as do all of the ferries.

LIQUOR LAWS   The legal age for purchase and consumption of alcoholic beverages is 21; proof of age is required and often requested at bars and restaurants. Do not carry open containers of alcohol in your car or any public area that isn't zoned for alcohol consumption. And nothing will ruin your trip faster than getting a citation for DUI ("driving under the influence"), so don't even think about driving while intoxicated.

LOST & FOUND   Be sure to tell all of your credit card companies the minute you discover your wallet has been lost or stolen and file a report at a police precinct. Your credit card company or insurer may require a police report number or record of the loss. Most credit card companies have an emergency toll-free number to call if your card is lost or stolen. **Visa**'s U.S. emergency number is ☎ 800/847-2911 or 410/581-9994. **American Express** cardholders and traveler's check holders should call ☎ 800/221-7282. **MasterCard** holders should call ☎ **800/307-7309** or 636/722-7111. For other credit cards, call the toll-free number directory at ☎ **800/555-1212.** You can have money wired to you via Western Union (☎ 800/325-6000; www.westernunion.com).

MAIL & POSTAGE   At press time, domestic postage rates were 26¢ for a postcard and 42¢ for a letter. For international mail, a first-class letter of up to 1 ounce costs 90¢ (69¢ to Canada and Mexico); a first-class postcard costs 90¢ (69¢ to Canada and Mexico). For more information go to www.usps.com and click on "Calculate Postage."

NEWSPAPERS & MAGAZINES   The *Seattle Post-Intelligencer* and *Seattle Times* are Seattle's two daily newspapers. *Seattle Weekly* is the city's free arts-and-entertainment weekly.

PHARMACIES   Conveniently located downtown pharmacies include **Rite Aid,** with branches at 319 Pike St. (☎ 206/223-0512) and 2603 Third Ave. (☎ 206/441-8790). For 24-hour service, try **Bartell Drug Store,** 600 First Ave. N. (☎ 206/284-1353).

POLICE   For police emergencies, phone ☎ 911.

RESTROOMS   There are public restrooms in **Pike Place Market, Westlake Center, Pacific Place, Seattle Center,** and the **Washington State Convention and Trade Center.** You'll also find restrooms in most hotel lobbies and coffee bars in downtown Seattle.

SAFETY   Although Seattle is a relatively safe city, it has its share of crime. The most questionable neighborhood you're likely to visit is the Pioneer Square area. By day, this area is quite safe (though it has a large contingent of street people), but when the bars are closing, stay aware of your surroundings. Also take extra precautions with your wallet or purse when you're in the crush of people at Pike Place Market. Try to park your car in a garage at night. If you must park on the street, make sure there are no valuables in view.

SMOKING   Smoking is banned in public indoor spaces throughout the state of Washington, even in bars.

TAXES   Seattle has an 8.8% sales tax. In restaurants, there's an additional .5% food-and-beverage tax. The hotel-room tax in the metro area ranges from around 10% to 16%. On rental cars, you pay an 18.6% tax, plus, if you rent at the airport, a 10% to 12% airport concession fee (plus other fees for a whopping total of around 45%!).

TELEPHONES   Hotel surcharges can be astronomical, so use your cellphone or a public pay telephone. Many convenience groceries sell prepaid calling cards; for international visitors these can be the least expensive way to call home. Many public pay phones at airports now accept American Express, MasterCard, and Visa credit cards. For calls within the United States and to Canada, dial 1 followed by the area code and the seven-digit number. For other international calls, dial 011 followed by the country code, city code, and the number you are calling.

Calls to area codes 800, 888, 877, and 866 are toll-free. For local directory assistance ("information"), dial 411; for long-distance information, dial 1, then the appropriate area code and 555-1212.

TIME   The continental United States is divided into four time zones: Eastern Standard Time (EST), Central Standard Time (CST), Mountain Standard Time (MST), and Pacific Standard Time (PST). Alaska and Hawaii have their own zones. For example, when it's 9am in Los Angeles (PST), it's 7am in Honolulu (HST), 10am in Denver (MST), 11am in Chicago (CST), noon in New York

City (EST), 5pm in London (GMT), and 2am the next day in Sydney. Seattle is on Pacific Standard Time (PST), making it 3 hours behind the East Coast.

Daylight saving time is in effect from 1am on the second Sunday in March to 1am on the first Sunday in November, except in Arizona, Hawaii, the U.S. Virgin Islands, and Puerto Rico. Daylight saving time moves the clock 1 hour ahead of standard time.

TIPPING Tips are the standard way of showing appreciation for services provided. In hotels, tip bellhops at least $1 per bag ($2–$3 if you have a lot of luggage) and tip the chamber staff $1 to $2 per day (more if you've left a disaster area). Tip the doorman or concierge only if he or she has provided you with some specific service. Tip the valet-parking attendant $1 every time you get your car. In restaurants, bars, and nightclubs, tip service staff 15% to 20% of the check, tip bartenders 10% to 15%, tip checkroom attendants $1 per garment, and tip valet-parking attendants $1 per vehicle. Tip cab drivers 15% of the fare; tip skycaps at airports at least $1 per bag ($2–$3 if you have a lot of luggage); and tip hairdressers and barbers 15% to 20%.

TRANSIT INFO For 24-hour information on Seattle's **Metro** bus system, call ☎ **800/542-7876** in Washington, or ☎ 206/553-3000, or go to http://transit.metrokc.gov. For information on the **Washington State Ferries,** call ☎ **800/843-3779** or

888/808-7977 in Washington or 206/464-6400, or go to www.wsdot.wa.gov/ferries.

TRAVELERS WITH DISABILITIES For anyone using a wheelchair, the greatest difficulty of a visit to Seattle is dealing with the city's steep hills. One solution for dealing with downtown hills is to use the elevator at Pike Place Market to get between the waterfront and First Avenue. There's also a public elevator at the west end of Lenora Street (just north of Pike Place Market). This elevator connects the waterfront with the Belltown neighborhood. If you stay at The Edgewater hotel, right on the waterfront, you'll have easy access to all of the city's waterfront attractions, and you'll be able to use the elevators to get to Pike Place Market.

Organizations that offer assistance to disabled travelers include **MossRehab** (☎ **800/CALL-MOSS;** www.mossresourcenet.org); the **American Foundation for the Blind** (AFB; ☎ **800/232-5463;** www.afb.org); and **SATH** (Society for Accessible Travel & Hospitality; ☎ **212/447-7284;** www.sath.org). **AirAmbulanceCard.com** is now partnered with SATH and allows you to preselect top-notch hospitals in case of an emergency.

WEATHER Check the *Seattle Times* or *Seattle Post-Intelligencer* newspapers for forecasts. If you want to know what to pack before you depart, go to www.wrh.noaa.gov/seattle, www.cnn.com/weather, or www.wunderground.com/US/WA.

Seattle: **A Brief History**

1792 British explorer George Vancouver arrives and names the Puget Sound.

1851 The Denny party makes land at Alki Point (now West Seattle) and endures a harsh first winter with the help of native tribes.

1852 Denny and gang move their town to the more temperate east side of the Puget Sound; "Doc" Maynard names the town after Chief Sealth (aka Chief Seattle) of the local Duwamish tribe.

1853 The Washington Territory is officially created; it includes what is now Idaho and part of Montana.

1853 Henry Yesler opens the first of many sawmills to be built in the Puget Sound area.

1855 The U.S. government signs treaties with several Native American tribes in the Washington Territory, giving much of their land to the federal government.

1861 The University of Washington (then called Territorial University) opens its doors.

1863 Idaho Territory is separated from the Washington Territory.

1863 The *Gazette,* later to become the *Seattle Post-Intelligencer,* publishes its first edition.

1864 Cross-country Western Union telegraph line reaches Seattle.

1869 The City of Seattle incorporates.

1871 The Indian Appropriations Act says Native Americans are no longer sovereign but federal "wards."

1878 Seattle gets its first telephones.

1885 Chinese immigrants are forced out of Seattle.

1889 Twenty-five blocks of Seattle burn to the ground in the Great Fire, prompting a frenzy of building—several feet above where the original shops had been.

1889 Washington becomes the nation's 42nd state.

1893 Transcontinental Great Northern Railway reaches Seattle.

1896 Col. Alden Blethen buys the *Seattle Daily Times.* (The Blethen family still owns the *Seattle Times.*)

1897–99 Seattle booms as a stopping-off point for Klondike gold-seekers.

1901 John Nordstrom opens his first shoe store.

1907 Pike Place Market brings farmers and customers directly together.

1910 Seattle women win their on-again-off-again right to vote once and for all.

1914 Smith Tower is completed in Seattle, becoming the tallest building west of Ohio.

1915 William Boeing goes for his first flight.

1916 A long, violent longshoremen's strike takes place.

1917 Construction is complete on the Lake Washington Ship Canal.

1917 Boeing Airplane Co. is launched.

1919 The nation's first general strike causes mayhem in Seattle.

1919 First international airmail delivery by Boeing and Hubbard.

1919 Eddie Bauer's first store opens.

1921 The Alien Land Law is passed in Washington, restricting Asian immigrants' rights to own or lease property.

1924 Native Americans are made U.S. citizens.

1926 Seattle elects the first woman mayor of any major U.S. city.

1940 Lake Washington Floating Bridge becomes the first of its kind in the world.

1940 Sen. Henry "Scoop" Jackson wins election to Congress, and later to the U.S. Senate.

1942 FDR signs order sending Japanese Americans from the West Coast to internment camps; thousands in the Seattle area are forced to abandon their homes and businesses.

1942 Seattle native Jimi Hendrix is born.

1949 Sea-Tac International Airport opens.

1951 Washington State Ferries begin service on the Puget Sound.

1954 First successful passenger jet, the Boeing 707, takes off.

1962 Seattle builds Space Needle and monorail for the World's Fair.

1966 Boeing builds the first 747 assembly plant.

1970s Boeing layoffs devastate the local economy.

1971 Starbucks opens its first shop, and the rest is history.

1975 Microsoft is founded by Bill Gates and Paul Allen in Albuquerque, NM; 3 years later it moves to the Seattle area.

1976 The first woman governor of Washington, Dixy Lee Ray, is elected.

1976 The new Seahawks football team plays its first game.

1977 The new Mariners baseball team throws its first pitch.

1979 The Seattle SuperSonics win the NBA Championship.

1999 A World Trade Organization conference in downtown Seattle prompts riots, property damage, and accusations of police misconduct.

2001 The Nisqually Earthquake causes extensive damage to many older Seattle buildings.

2004 Washington elects Christine Gregoire in tightest governor's race in U.S. history, giving the state three women in its top political positions—two U.S. senators and the governor.

2005 Smoking is banned in all public places in Washington.

2006 Starbucks CEO Howard Schultz sells the Seattle SuperSonics team to an Oklahoma group after the city refuses to expand the basketball arena or build a new one. This leaves the Sonics' future in Seattle in doubt.

2007 The Washington state Legislature legalizes same-sex unions. ●

Index

See also Accommodations and Restaurant indexes, below.

Photo **Credits**

p viii: © William Sutton/DanitaDelimont.com; p 4, bottom: © Walter Bibikow/DanitaDelimont.com; p 5, top: © Joseph Sohm/Visions of America, LLC/Alamy; p 5, bottom: © Charles Crust/Danita Delimont/Alamy; p 6, top: © John Burke/AGE Fotostock; p 6, bottom: © Howard Frisk; p 7: © Walter Bibikow/AGE Fotostock; p 9, center: © Wim Wiskerke/Alamy; p 10, top: © Howard Frisk; p 11, top: © Howard Frisk; p 13, bottom: © Howard Frisk; p 14, top: © Chris Cheadle/AGE Fotostock; p 14, bottom: © Mark Gibson/Photolibrary; p 15, top left: © Howard Frisk; p 15, top right: © Scott Pitts/dk/Alamy; p 17, bottom: © Wolfgang Kaehler/Alamy; p 18, bottom: © William Sutton/DanitaDelimont.com; p 19: © Charles Crust/Danita Delimont/Alamy; p 22, top: © Howard Frisk; p 23, bottom: © Richard Cummins/Lonely Planet Images; p 24, top: Courtesy Wing Luke Asian Museum; p 25, bottom: © Richard Cummins/Lonely Planet Images; p 27, top: © Howard Frisk; p 27, bottom: © Scott Pitts/dk/Alamy; p 28, bottom: © Howard Frisk; p 29, top: © Chuck Pefley/Alamy; p 29, bottom: © Jamie And Judy Wild/DanitaDelimont.com; p 31, center: Courtesy Landmark Theatres; p 32, top: © Dick Busher/The 5th Avenue Theatre; p 33, top: Courtesy ACT Theatre; p 33, bottom: Courtesy Paramount Theatre; p 35, top: © John Elk III/Lonely Planet Images; p 35, bottom: © Chris Bennion/Seattle Children's Theatre; p 36, bottom: © Howard Frisk; p 37, top: © Chuck Pefley/Alamy; p 37, bottom: © Zach Holmes/Alamy; p 39, center: © Scott Pitts/dk/Alamy; p 39, bottom: © Pat Canova/Alamy; p 40, bottom: © Ann Cutting/Alamy; p 41, top: © Richard Cummins/SuperStock; p 41, bottom: © Chuck Pefley/Alamy; p 43, center: © David Zimmerman/Masterfile; p 43, bottom: © Chris Howes/Wild Places Photography/Alamy; p 44, top: © Jamie And Judy Wild/DanitaDelimont.com; p 45, bottom: © Randy Faris/Corbis; p 46, top: © Lawrence Worcester/Lonely Planet Images; p 46, bottom: © Howard Frisk; p 47, top: © Charles Crust/DanitaDelimont.com; p 48, top: © Ed Gifford/Masterfile; p 48, bottom: © Richard Cummins/Lonely Planet Images; p 49: © Charles Crust/DanitaDelimont.com; p 51, bottom: © Howard Frisk; p 52, bottom: © Pat Canova/Alamy; p 53, top: © John And Lisa Merrill/DanitaDelimont.com; p 55, bottom: © Lauren Zeid/eStock Photo; p 56, bottom: © Howard Frisk; p 57, top: © dk/Alamy; p 57, bottom: © Dave Bartruff/DanitaDelimont.com; p 58, center: © Mike Dobel/Masterfile; p 58, bottom: © Lauren Zeid/eStock Photo; p 59, top: © Scott Pitts/dk/Alamy; p 59, bottom: © Lawrence Worcester/Lonely Planet Images; p 61, bottom: © Scott Pitts/dk/Alamy; p 62, top: © Lawrence Worcester/Lonely Planet Images; p 63, bottom: © Howard Frisk; p 64, top: © Ed Rooney/Alamy; p 65, top: © Rod Crow/Alamy; p 65, bottom: © Rod Crow/Alamy; p 67, center: © Douglas H. Orton/drr.net; p 67, bottom: © John Elk III/Lonely Planet Images; p 68, top: © Howard Frisk; p 68, bottom: © Howard Frisk; p 69, top: Courtesy Seattle Museum of the Mysteries; p 71, bottom: © Greg Vaughn/Alamy; p 72, top: © Howard Frisk; p 72, bottom: © Howard Frisk; p 73, top: © Howard Frisk; p 75, top: © Patrick Bennett/drr.net; p 75, bottom: © Chuck Pefley/Alamy; p 76, top: © Lawrence Worcester/Lonely Planet Images; p 77: © Howard Frisk; p 78, bottom: © Howard Frisk; p 83, center: © Howard Frisk; p 83, bottom: © Howard Frisk; p 84, top: © Howard Frisk; p 85, bottom: © Howard Frisk; p 86, top: © Howard Frisk; p 86, bottom: © Howard Frisk; p 87, top: © Howard Frisk; p 88, bottom: © Howard Frisk; p 89, top: © Howard Frisk; p 89, bottom: © Howard Frisk; p 90, top: © Howard Frisk; p 91, bottom: © Howard Frisk; p 92, bottom: © Howard Frisk; p 93: © David A. Barnes/Alamy; p 95, bottom: © Douglas Lander/Alamy; p 97, top: © Michele Westmorland/DanitaDelimont.com; p 97, bottom: © Jamie And Judy Wild/DanitaDelimont.com; p 98, bottom: © Chris Howes/Wild Places Photography/Alamy; p 99, top: © Douglas H. Orton/drr.net; p 99, bottom: © John And Lisa Merrill/Danita Delimont/Alamy; p 101, top: © Howard Frisk; p 101, bottom: © Howard Frisk; p 103, top: © Charles Crust/DanitaDelimont.com; p 103, bottom: © Howard Frisk; p 105, top: © Lwilk I Dreamstime.com; p 105, bottom: © John Elk III/Lonely Planet Images; p 107, bottom: © Howard Frisk; p 108, bottom: © Charles Crust/DanitaDelimont.com; p 109: Courtesy The Westin Seattle; p 110, bottom: © Howard Frisk; p 115, bottom: © Howard Frisk; p 116, bottom: © Howard Frisk; p 117, top: Courtesy Canlis Restaurant; p 118, top: © Howard Frisk; p 119, bottom: © Howard Frisk; p 120, top: © Howard Frisk; p 121, top: © Howard Frisk; p 121, bottom: © Lawrence Worcester/Lonely Planet Images; p 122, bottom: Courtesy The Edgewater; p 124, top: © Howard Frisk; p 125: © Jake Warga/Danita Delimont/Alamy; p 126, bottom: © Howard Frisk; p 130, bottom: © Lawrence Worcester/Lonely

Planet Images; p 131, top: © Howard Frisk; p 131, bottom: © Howard Frisk; p 132, bottom: © Howard Frisk; p 133, top: © Howard Frisk; p 134, bottom: © Howard Frisk; p 135: © William Anthony/Teatro ZinZanni; p 136, bottom: © Angela Sterling/Courtesy Pacific Northwest Ballet; p 138, bottom: © Howard Frisk; p 139, top: Courtesy Yuen Lui Studio; p 139, bottom: © Angela Sterling/Courtesy Pacific Northwest Ballet; p 140, bottom: © Fabio Marino/Teatro ZinZanni; p 141, top: © Rozarii Lynch/Seattle Opera; p 141, bottom: © Howard Frisk; p 142, top: © Howard Frisk; p 142, bottom: © Chris Bennion/Courtesy ACT Theatre; p 143: Courtesy W Seattle; p 146, bottom: Courtesy The Edgewater; p 148, top: Courtesy Fairmont Olympic Hotel; p 149, bottom: Courtesy Hotel Monaco; p 150, bottom: © Howard Frisk; p 151, top: Courtesy W Seattle; p 152, bottom: Courtesy The Westin Seattle; p 153: © Stuart Westmorland/DanitaDelimont.com; p 155, bottom: © Zach Holmes/Alamy; p 157, bottom: © Trish Drury/DanitaDelimont.com; p 159, bottom: © Jamie And Judy Wild/Danita Delimont.com; p 161, center: © Ulana Switucha/Alamy; p 162, top: © Gunter Marx/Alamy; p 162, bottom: © Gonzalo Azumendi/AGE Fotostock; p 163: © Chris Cheadle/AGE Fotostock

The new way to get AROUND town.

Make the most of your stay. Go Day by Day

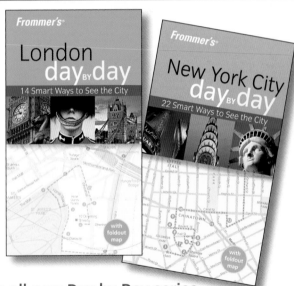

The all-new Day by Day series shows you the best places to visit and the best way to see them.

- Full-color throughout, with hundreds of photos and maps
- Packed with 1–to–3–day itineraries, neighborhood walks, and thematic tours
- Museums, literary haunts, offbeat places, and more
- Star-rated hotel and restaurant listings
- Sturdy foldout map in reclosable plastic wallet
- Foldout front covers with at-a-glance maps and info

The best trips start here.

Frommer's®
A Branded Imprint of ⓦWILEY
Now you know.

Wiley and the Wiley logo are registered trademarks of John Wiley & Sons, Inc. Frommer's is a registered trademark of Arthur Frommer.